O COME EMMANUEL

A MUSICAL TOUR OF DAILY READINGS FOR ADVENT AND CHRISTMAS

GORDON GILES

PARACLETE PRESS
BREWSTER, MASSACHUSETTS

O *Come Emmanuel: A Musical Tour of Daily Readings for Advent and Christmas*

2006 First Printing, Paraclete Press Edition

Copyright © 2006 Gordon Giles

ISBN 10: 1-55725-515-6
ISBN 13: 978-1-55725-515-0
Originally published in 2005 by The Bible Reading Fellowship, Oxford, England.

Library of Congress Cataloging-in-Publication Data

Giles, Gordon, 1966-
  O come Emmanuel : a musical tour of daily readings for Advent
and Christmas / Gordon Giles.—1st Paraclete Press ed.
      p. cm.
  Originally published: Oxford, England : Bible Reading Fellowship, 2005.
  ISBN 1-55725-515-6
  1. Advent Meditations. 2. Christmas—Meditations. 3. Advent
hymns—Meditations. 4. Christmas—Meditations.
  5. Bible—Meditations. 6. Devotional calendars. I. Title.
  BV40.G55 2006
  242'.33—dc22
                                    2006022708

10 9 8 7 6 5 4 3 2 1

Published by Paraclete Press
Brewster, Massachusetts
www.paracletepress.com
Printed in the United States of America

Contents

Introduction

C hristmas is about the birth of Christ, even though there are people who do not know this, have forgotten it, or want to make it mean something different. And we have very little excuse for not knowing what Christmas is about, because so much of the music that we encounter at this time of year tells and interprets the events of the nativity in song.

Singing carols or attending concerts can be great fun, and for many, Christmas simply isn't Christmas without doing so. But Christmas is not about carols: carols are about Christmas!

Carols can teach and show us a great deal about our faith and can help us in our pilgrimage through life, reminding, cajoling, and inspiring us to take the incarnation of Jesus seriously and to live our lives in the marvelous light of the love that God shows us by sending Jesus to us as savior. Over the next few weeks, we will explore some of the Christmas music that we hear all too often, and some that may be unfamiliar. Whatever the scope or duration of the work, the music says something to us about the text and the text helps us understand what is going on musically. When the text is a sacred text (from the Bible or a prayer book), there comes into play another, deeper dimension as the composer tries to combine words and music either to praise God or to say something about God, or both. Day by day, using Advent and Christmas music, we will strive to magnify the wonders of God revealed in Jesus Christ, who is judge, redeemer, promised savior, suffering servant, anointed one, king of glory, child of Bethlehem, Son of Man, Word made flesh, light of the world, lamb of God, incarnate Son of God.

We will meet Christians from the past, and living poets and musicians of faith. In their words we find profound spiritual insight but also sometimes questionable theology, mystical wonder, and pagan influence. We will dance with Christ, and walk with the wise men. We will travel to Turkey, Italy, Sweden, Germany, France, and Spain on our route to the cradle at Bethlehem. And then we will flee from Herod to Coventry, although our apparently bleak midwinter will still be warmed by the sun of righteousness.

We will delve into Testaments Old and New, and manuscripts ancient and modern, in search of the truth from above. We will have fun and games with 12 partridges, 22 turtle doves, 30 French hens, 36 calling birds, 40 gold rings, 42 laying geese, 42 swans, 40 milk-maids, 36 dancing girls, 30 lords, 22 pipers and 12 drummers eventually in attendance! We will hear of selfless sacrifice, charity and love, of forgiveness, reconciliation, and hope; yet we will also face the realities of death and judgment, pain and loss, crime and punishment, anticipation and disappointment, darkness and light. With Scripture and song, we will pray with confidence and fear, sorrow and joy, for others and ourselves. And, as is inevitable at this time of year, we will remember all those whom we love but see no longer, mindful of the fragility of human existence and the vastness of creation.

While Advent, Christmas, and Epiphany are very much part of our Christian heritage, having something of a Christian tradition and being familiar with and appreciative of it are not the same thing. In this book we can examine only a small part of the heritage of faith that forms the structure upon which these seasons are piled. Of course there are omissions: the season is simply not long enough to enable us to enjoy the full fare that is offered.

Nevertheless, it is my hope and prayer that this musical mystery tour of Advent and Christmas will help and inspire all of us to re-examine and notice what we sing and hear at this time of year.

As we venture into the season of Advent, and from there to Christmas and Epiphany, accompanied by a diverse group of musicians and poets, let us look for inspiration, hope, solace, and encouragement and remember that our ultimate desire is the praise of God, creator Father, incarnate Son, and living Spirit, not only at this time of year, but always.

The Advent responsory

"When the Son of Man comes in his glory, and all the angels with him,
then he will sit on the throne of his glory. All the nations will be gathered
before him, and he will separate people one from another as a shepherd
separates the sheep from the goats, and he will put the sheep at his
right hand and the goats at the left.... Then he will say to those at his
left hand, 'You that are accursed, depart from me into the eternal fire
prepared for the devil and his angels; for I was hungry and you gave
me no food, I was thirsty and you gave me nothing to drink, I was a
stranger and you did not welcome me, naked and you did not give me
clothing, sick and in prison and you did not visit me.' Then they also
will answer, 'Lord, when was it that we saw you hungry or thirsty or a
stranger or naked or sick or in prison, and did not take care of you?'
Then he will answer them, 'Truly I tell you, just as you did not do it to
one of the least of these, you did not do it to me.' And these will go away
into eternal punishment, but the righteous into eternal life."
—Matthew 25:31–33, 41–46

I look from afar:
And lo, I see the power of God coming,
and a cloud covering the whole earth.
Go ye out to meet him and say:
Tell us, art thou he that should come to reign over thy people
Israel?
High and low, rich and poor, one with another,
Go ye out to meet him and say:
Hear, O thou shepherd of Israel, thou that leadest Joseph like a
sheep:
Tell us, art thou he that should come?
Stir up thy strength, O Lord, and come
To reign over thy people Israel.

Glory be to the Father, and to the Son, and to the Holy Ghost.
I look from afar, and lo, I see the power of God coming, and a cloud covering the whole earth.
Go ye out to meet him and say:
Tell us, art thou he that should come to reign over thy people Israel?

Words: The First Matins Responsory for Advent Sunday
Music: adapted from G.P. da Palestrina (c. 1525–94)

The singing of this responsory at the beginning of an Advent carol service on the first Sunday of Advent marks the beginning of the December season of penitence, anticipation, and hope. The words and music are derived from the doxology and chanted portions from the odd verses of the Magnificat by Palestrina (the Bible text of the Magnificat is Luke 1:46–55). The responsory text itself comes from the old Latin service of Matins (Morning Prayer). The version that has become popular through use at places such as King's College Chapel, Cambridge, has harmonized responses.

This simple opening to Advent points us toward the return of Christ as judge and king, reigning over the whole earth, but also judging the whole earth, as the parable of the sheep and goats suggests.

The Bible says that when we die we are judged. Advent is the distinctive season for reflecting on the last judgment, which Matthew describes in the parable of the sheep and the goats. In that parable we are presented with a kingly Christ as judge. This means that it is his criteria, not ours, that form the basis of that judgment. It is Christ who has the power, not us, and this actually means that he can do whatever he likes, but not in the sense that we can think what we "like" when it comes to death and judgment. We believe that God was in Christ reconciling the world to himself, offering forgiveness, rescuing us from sin, and preparing a place for us in heaven. Therefore we have to acknowledge that when Christ sits on his heavenly throne, he can, and perhaps will, be very merciful indeed.

It would not be truly biblical of us to confine ourselves to an image of Christ sitting on a throne wielding absolute power. Christ is powerful, of course, but the Gospels are not a catalogue of his exercising worldly, judgmental power. They are rather accounts of how he shows that he has power, and, through his ministry, how he gently, bravely, and willingly lays it down. We are shown, in the account of his temptations in the wilderness (Matthew 4:1–11), that Jesus had the power to be a very different kind of king—a tyrant who exercises absolute authority, governing through fear and the suppression of any alternative. But he rejected that approach, and it is fundamental to Christianity that we have a choice. Our king forces no allegiance from us, but frees us to love him, or not to do so.

In his earthly ministry, Jesus demonstrates his power to heal: cleansing lepers, casting out demons, curing the sick and lame. We also see Jesus' intellectual power. He tells parables and con-founds the religious leaders of his time both by asking awkward questions of his own and by evading theirs. Whether it is tax to Caesar or the fate of a sinner, Jesus conquers their cunning and prejudice. This also reveals his moral power, as does the idea that he is sinless, both in character and action.

As we consider the end of Jesus' ministry, we realize, as his disciples do, that this is the Messiah, in whom all things were made, whose name is above all names in this age and in every age to come. Yet, as soon as we realize this, we see it all slip away. Betrayal, arrest, trials, torture, execution all follow in swift succession. Where has his power gone? He has laid it down—surrendered it to human hatred. He, who is characterized as the Son of Man judging humans like sheep and goats, allows himself to be humanly judged, falsely convicted, and killed.

This kind of kingship and this kind of love are unique in history. This is the love of Christ, which inverts itself for the benefit of others, truly nourishing others. This kingship and this love are both about self-giving and the laying down of worldly power. That is why, if we want to think of Christ as a king, we must think of him not only as judge but primarily as the king of love. And it is the king of love whose return we anticipate and desire, not just in Advent, but at all times.

Prayer

As Advent begins, O Lord Christ, come again to reign over your people and enlighten all nations. Have mercy on all who look to you, and hasten that day when your justice and love will be revealed for the good of all creation and the glory of God the Father, with whom and the Spirit you are sovereign in majesty and power. Amen.

Come, Thou Redeemer of the earth

For a child has been born for us, a son given to us; authority rests upon his shoulders; and he is named Wonderful Counselor, Mighty God, Everlasting Father, Prince of Peace. His authority shall grow continually, and there shall be endless peace for the throne of David and his kingdom. He will establish and uphold it with justice and with righteousness from this time onwards and for evermore. The zeal of the Lord of hosts will do this.
—Isaiah 9:6–7

Come, Thou Redeemer of the earth,
And manifest Thy virgin birth:
Let every age adoring fall;
Such birth befits the God of all.
Begotten of no human will,
But of the Spirit, Thou art still
The Word of God in flesh arrayed,
The promised Fruit to man displayed.
The virgin womb that burden gained
With virgin honor all unstained;
The banners there of virtue glow;
God in His temple dwells below.

Forth from His chamber goeth He,
That royal home of purity,
A giant in twofold substance one,
Rejoicing now His course to run.
From God the Father He proceeds,
To God the Father back He speeds;
His course He runs to death and hell,

Returning on God's throne to dwell.
O equal to the Father, Thou!
Gird on Thy fleshly mantle now;
The weakness of our mortal state
With deathless might invigorate.
Thy cradle here shall glitter bright,
And darkness breathe a newer light,
Where endless faith shall shine serene,
And twilight never intervene.
All laud to God the Father be,
All praise, eternal Son, to Thee;
All glory, as is ever meet,
To God the Holy Paraclete.

Words: Ambrose of Milan (340–397), trans. John Mason Neale (1818–66)
Music: VENI REDEMPTOR plainsong Mode 1
PUER NOBIS NASCITUR Trier manuscript, 15th century

"Come, Thou Redeemer of the earth" often follows the Advent Responsory, which we considered yesterday. Often the responsory is sung at the west end of the church, and then the choir proceed eastward, singing this straightforward tune. It is a very effective way to open a service, with music and movement. As the choir walks eastward, they are walking in the direction of Jerusalem, toward the chamber of salvation, the "royal home" from which the Father sends his Spirit-begotten Son. Such a progression sets the scene for what is to follow: words and song telling forth the Advent promise of hope and light.

This carol is, as they say, one of the oldest ones in the book. Its author, Ambrose of Milan, was not actually Italian but was born in Augusta Trevorum, which was then in Gaul (France), and is now known as Trier, in Germany. Hence he was a Roman citizen, who followed his father into a career in politics, being made governor of Aemilia-Liguria (northern Italy) around 370. When the bishop of Milan died in 374, the local lay people wanted Ambrose to succeed him. There was a major problem: Ambrose, while a believer, had not actually been ordained, or even baptized. After much soul-searching, he accepted the bishopric, and was hastily baptized and ordained. He became famous for his preaching and his role in the conversion of Augustine of Hippo (354–430). He wrote treatises on ethics and on the sacraments, and some have even attributed the Athanasian creed to his pen. He is revered as a saint and a "doctor" of the church. His feast day is December 7 in both Roman Catholic and Anglican calendars.

This hymn, known originally in Latin as *Veni, Redemptor gentium,* dates from 397, the last year of Ambrose's life, and was brought into English use by the Victorian poet and translator J. M. Neale, who, in his short life, made a very significant contribution to English hymnody. "Good King Wenceslas" is one of his own compositions, but he is better known for his many hundred translations from Latin and Greek. As we proceed into Advent, with Christmas as our destination, it is good to have a sketch map of the terrain ahead. And what a reminder! Here in microcosm we have the desire of nations expressed: "Come, Redeemer of the earth" and the anticipation of the virgin birth at Bethlehem, both in the first verse. We are reminded that the incarnate Christ, although born at a point in space and time, is still the Son of God. Christ reigns in glory as the Word made flesh, and dwells among us today in the ministry of the Holy Spirit. Ambrose refers to Christ as the "promised fruit," a lovely description that recalls the "forbidden fruit" that tempts Adam and Eve, but that also hails Christ as the promised Savior anticipated by Isaiah and in the Psalms. Christ, the second Adam, turns forbidden fruit into promised fruit, fulfilling the pages of prophecy and bringing release to all those who, like the first Adam, are bound by sin.

The use of the word "fruit" is also reminiscent of the description of Jesus as "fruit of the womb of Mary" (Luke 1:42), and Ambrose writes of Jesus "coming forth" from the chamber that is his mother's womb, the "royal place of purity." Thus, from her is born a child, both human and divine. The fourth-century poetry is earthy and earthly, but in being so it combines the mystery of incarnation with the real presence of human birth.

In this rich passage of poetry there is much condensed, so that only hints of Isaiah's words of promise can be detected. Ambrose's deep theological insight encapsulates the promise and realization of salvation in Christ, whose birth is foreseen in Isaiah 9 and described in Luke 1–2. Thus his hymn is a treatise in itself, to which he brings a lifetime of spiritual study and pastoral wisdom. In this one hymn, he succeeds in doing something to which we devote the whole Advent carol service: unpacking the prophetic meaning of Old Testament passages and the gradual realization that they point to and predict the birth and ministry of Christ.

Prayer

O Lord our redeemer, whose incarnation manifests the love of the Father revealed in human flesh, breathe a new light upon your world, that the weakness of our mortality might be invigorated by your power and glory, until that day when all nations will bow down before your throne, on which you reign, Father, Son, and Holy Spirit, now and for ever. Amen.

Then the seventh angel blew his trumpet, and there were loud voices in heaven, saying, "The kingdom of the world has become the kingdom of our Lord and of his Messiah, and he will reign for ever and ever." Then the twenty-four elders who sit on their thrones before God fell on their faces and worshiped God, singing, "We give you thanks, Lord God Almighty, who are and who were, for you have taken your great power and begun to reign. The nations raged, but your wrath has come, and the time for judging the dead, for rewarding your servants, the prophets and saints and all who fear your name, both small and great, and for destroying those who destroy the earth."
Revelation 11:15–18

Christ conquers,
Christ is King,
Christ is the Lord.
O Christ, hear us.
To the Holy Church of God, uniting
souls across the divisions of the nations: perpetual peace!
Christ conquers…
King of kings. Our King.
Our hope. Our glory.
O Christ, hear us.
To all leaders of the nations, and
those entrusted to their care;
honor unstained, life and victory.
O Christ, hear us.
O King of the nations, and their
desire, the Corner-stone,
who makest both one.

Christ conquers...
Our aid.
Our strength.
Our invincible shield.
Our impregnable wall.
Our light, our way, and our life.
O Christ, hear us.
O Emmanuel, our King and
lawgiver, the goal of all nations
and their Savior.
Christ conquers...
To him alone be the sovereignty,
praise and rejoicing, through
unending ages of ages. Amen.
May they have happiness,
Who are redeemed by the
blood of Christ! And joy!
May Christ's peace come!
May Christ's kingdom come!
Thanks be to God. Amen.

Laudes Regiae: Words and chant eleventh century (or earlier)

This very ancient piece of music was originally used in French monasteries and churches when the king attended worship. An early manuscript is associated with Osmund, who, as bishop of Salisbury in the eleventh century, completed the building of the cathedral there.

Osmund is credited with the "Ordinal of Offices," which, as the "Sarum Rite," became widely used as the primary liturgical service book throughout the south of England. The original is still preserved in Salisbury Cathedral. While the impact and meaning of "Christus vincit" is strong and regal, it can be both appealing and disturbing. In history it has been used to uphold and defend the power of kings, by allying their power to the power of Christ the King. How are we to understand or engage with the so-called kingship of Christ? There aren't very many kings to relate to these days, and while there are reigning kings in various countries, they are generally constitutional monarchs, having little real power, serving as symbolic heads of state. While the power of kings or queens is not something with which we are particularly familiar these days, we are very familiar with the concept of power, for all around us people are exercising power on many levels and in different contexts, for better or worse. Power is really all about change. The people in power are those who can bring about, or prevent, change. In order to do this, there can be exploitative power at play, where violence or threats are involved. There can also be manipulative power, such that the desire is to shape another person's or group's behavior to suit one's own ends. This can happen at international level or at a quiet, personal level. There is also competitive power—the kind of power that is often felt and wielded in playgrounds and board-rooms alike.

There are also positive models of power, such as integrative power, which is exercised in order to support or underscore another's power. Integrative power backs other people up, defends them and stands alongside them, in sickness or in health, for better or worse. Integrative power creates a positive power base that is mutual and often outward-looking. This is a kind of fellowship power—strength in numbers, the power of trust and teamwork. It is the kind of power that Jesus exercised throughout his ministry as he taught and trained the disciples to carry on his work and spread the gospel after his resurrection and ascension.

There is another positive form of power, which sociologists call "nutrient" power, which is power used on behalf of another's greater good. This sounds a bit like the power of love, the power of putting someone else first, or at least of putting one's own abilities, information, expertise, and desires at the service of others. This is the power of giving, both of self and of resources.

These are certainly not the models of power that the eleventh-century Norman conquerors or their clergy had in mind. Today, to help us toward a more contemporary way of understanding Christ's kingship, we can think of these two kinds of power—integrative and nutrient power—remembering that Christ's kingship is unique and is in some sense paradoxical. Christ certainly has power, but his sovereignty consists largely in the fact that he gave it up when he submitted himself to the human, destructive wills that put him on a cross to die. Christ's sovereignty consists in weakness, belying a greater power. And that greater power is the power of divine love—love revealed, love laid down, love spent.

Prayer
O Christ our King, shine your light on our souls, that we may reflect your love. Deepen our vision, that we may see you more clearly. Refine us like gold, that we may become pure in your sight. Touch our hearts and lives, that we may always act for your sake, in the power of your love, for you lived and died for us, but now reign in glory. Amen.

December 4   Lo! he comes with clouds descending

Blessed is the one who reads aloud the words of the prophecy, and blessed are those who hear and who keep what is written in it; for the time is near.

John to the seven churches that are in Asia: Grace to you and peace from him who is and who was and who is to come, and from the seven spirits who are before his throne, and from Jesus Christ, the faithful witness, the firstborn of the dead, and the ruler of the kings of the earth. To him who loves us and freed us from our sins by his blood, and made us to be a kingdom, priests serving his God and Father, to him be glory and dominion for ever and ever. Amen. Look! He is coming with the clouds; every eye will see him, even those who pierced him; and on his account all the tribes of the earth will wail. So it is to be. Amen. "I am the Alpha and the Omega," says the Lord God, who is and who was and who is to come, the Almighty.
—Revelation 1:3–8

Lo! he comes with clouds descending,
Once for favored sinners slain;
Thousand thousand saints attending
Swell the triumph of his train:
Alleluya!
God appears, on earth to reign.

Every eye shall now behold him
Robed in dreadful majesty;
Those who set at nought and sold him,
Pierced and nailed him to the tree,
Deeply wailing
Shall the true Messiah see.

Those dear tokens of his passion
Still his dazzling body bears,
Cause of endless exultation
To his ransomed worshipers:
With what rapture
Gaze we on those glorious scars!

Yea, Amen! let all adore thee,
High on thine eternal throne;
Savior, take the power and glory:
Claim the kingdom for thine own:
O come quickly!
Alleluya! Come, Lord, come!

Words: Charles Wesley (1707–88) and John Cennick (1718–55)
Music: HELMSLEY. Melody notated by Thomas Olivers (1725–99)

This hymn, so often associated with Advent and rarely sung outside this season, is not necessarily best considered as purely appropriate for Advent. The words include "Alleluya," a joyful outburst which some traditions exclude during Advent and Lent, as a somber gesture in keeping with the penitential flavor of the season. Thus it can be strange singing this hymn if we have "given up" alleluias for Advent! In other respects, though, this is an excellent Advent hymn, because it focuses on the second coming of Christ, which is often dwarfed by a pre-Christmas anticipation.

The opening lines are drawn from the book of Revelation and declare at the outset that this is no sugary Christmas carol but a hymn that relishes the return of our Lord. We are invited to look heavenwards, to see the promised Savior returning, just as John prophesied in Revelation 1:3, echoing Daniel 7:13–15. And as he descends, the throng of the redeemed sweeps down to accompany his return in glory to earth, and those who nailed Jesus to the cross will at last see him as he is, the true Messiah. As the Messiah returns to judge, this may well cause those who have rejected him to "wail deeply." The image is a strong one, and we are introduced here to a scene of glory and power, but also of tribulation, pain, and destruction. Such scenes are foretold by Jesus in Mark 13, Matthew 24, and Luke 21.

This apocalyptic element of Advent is one of the season's key themes. We live in a kind of middle time—a period after the incarnation, death, and resurrection of Jesus, when God sent his Son into the world to carry the burden and weight of sin, so that he might open his arms for us on the cross, but also those days before the great end-time, when God shall bring all together. The end of the world is not something we generally want to contemplate, even though a basic knowledge of solar science indicates a future time when life on earth will not be sustainable. We can live in denial of such a future, and reconcile ourselves to the fact that it probably won't affect you or me, but we cannot actually deny the reality of the end of the world, any more than we can deny its beginning.

ɿ ɿ ɿ

Widely sung as this hymn is, we can't help wondering how many people sing these words proclaiming the return of Christ, but lack any sense of the reality of such a proclamation. It is easy to sing about the return of Christ, but how much harder to believe it, and harder still to live in the light of passages of Scripture such as the opening verses of the book of Revelation, which proclaim the return of Christ, who was and is and is to come.

As we move into the Advent season ourselves, we might begin by considering how we react to these apocalyptic visions. Do we believe them? Do we act and speak as though this kind of second coming might actually happen? In our imaginations do we gaze with rapture on Christ's dazzling body, singing "Alleluia" and looking forward to the coming of his kingdom here on earth? And what do we feel about the possibility that it might happen tomorrow?

Prayer

Christ our true Messiah, we adore you, high on your eternal throne. Prepare us to accept that day when you claim your kingdom for your own, when you return in glory to confound all those who think of you as nothing more than an interesting historical figure. Come as judge, redeemer, and mercy-giver, so that all tears may be wiped away and all wailing turned to rapture, for you live and reign, in union with the Father and the Spirit, now and for ever. Amen.

Wait for the Lord

But you, beloved, are not in darkness, for that day to surprise you like a thief; for you are all children of light and children of the day; we are not of the night or of darkness. So then, let us not fall asleep as others do, but let us keep awake and be sober; for those who sleep sleep at night, and those who are drunk get drunk at night. But since we belong to the day, let us be sober, and put on the breastplate of faith and love, and for a helmet the hope of salvation. For God has destined us not for wrath but for obtaining salvation through our Lord Jesus Christ, who died for us, so that whether we are awake or asleep we may live with him. Therefore encourage one another and build up each other, as indeed you are doing.
—1 Thessalonians 5:4–11

Wait for the Lord, whose day is near,
Wait for the Lord, keep watch, take heart.

Words and music: Taizé Community

I n the church, we traditionally associate waiting with this season of Advent. It is a time for pausing on our fast and hectic journey through life. One of the most effective ways to experience a sense of our Lord's return—to "wait for the Lord"—comes through contemplative music and prayer. I'm sure it is no coincidence that the kind of gentle, repetitive, contemplative singing revived by the Taizé community in France has been successful and popular because it enables us to engage with our own waiting spaces. This can be true whether we listen to music at home or participate in services using this kind of music. Silence can be difficult to handle (some people definitely dislike it), but the music of Taizé has made a distinctive and vital contribution to the prayer lives of millions of people.

The Taizé community is not a commercial venture, nor does it insist upon a narrow doctrine to which its friends and members must adhere. Founded in wartime Burgundy by (Brother) Roger Schutz, a Swiss man who initially gave assistance to Jews fleeing Nazi Germany, the Taizé community grew after the war, spreading a message of reconciliation. By 1949, Roger had been ordained, and four Swiss and three French men took vows of celibacy, poverty, and obedience, joining the community. Committed to ecumenical relations (the breaking down of divisions among Christian denominations), the Taizé community became popular with young people. Taizé is a place distinguished by its freedoms of spirit, fellowship, and language, and most of all by its sense of community, which, although located firmly in France, is easily translatable to other places and contexts.

"Wait for the Lord" reminds us of another dimension of waiting that is typical of the Taizé approach to life and faith, for instead of excitement, fear, and anticipation, there is also gentle acceptance and harmonious patience as we wait for the Lord. We have been waiting a long time, repeating the same basic melody, yet perhaps embellishing it creatively, so that our interest, our desire, and our love are not wearied. The way Taizé chants are sung involves continuity and repetition combined with creativity and personality, expressed in communal worship. A simple melody is harmonized in a fairly straightforward way, which means that through repetition even inexpert singers can learn their own part in the greater musical whole. Sometimes "canons" are used: divided groups sing the same tune a few notes apart, so that the melody keeps entering over again and the music seems overlaid, every part harmonizing with every other part.

The simple but effective approach to communal music and prayer both speaks to and reflects today's age in a beautifully integrated way. Each time we participate in a Taizé chant, we are involving ourselves in a stationary time with God, waiting for God and waiting with God. When we emerge from such an experience, we find that while time appears to have stood still, held in musical check by mutual melody, we ourselves have made a little journey towards God, accompanied by the Holy Spirit.

In this time of waiting, we have an opportunity to reject the here-and-now of present living and engage with God over time, forming a deep and extended relationship, in the heart of which we can search and be searched out, know and be known. We not only wait for God, we wait with God. To do that takes time, but we do have time. Let us not waste it or lose it, for one day, inevitably, we will run out of time.

Prayer
God of day and night, keep us vigilant in faith and patient in praise, until that great day when Christ returns in clouds of glory to lift us to your heavenly throne. Amen.

December 6   St. Nicholas

The saying is sure: whoever aspires to the office of bishop desires a noble task. Now a bishop must be above reproach, married only once, temperate, sensible, respectable, hospitable, an apt teacher, not a drunkard, not violent but gentle, not quarrelsome, and not a lover of money. He must manage his own household well, keeping his children submissive and respectful in every way—for if someone does not know how to manage his own household, how can he take care of God's church? He must not be a recent convert, or he may be puffed up with conceit and fall into the condemnation of the devil. Moreover, he must be well thought of by outsiders, so that he may not fall into disgrace and the snare of the devil.
—1 Timothy 3:1–7

God moves in a mysterious way
His wonders to perform;
He plants his footsteps in the sea,
And rides upon the storm.

Deep in unfathomable mines
Of never-failing skill
He treasures up his bright designs,
And works his sovereign will.

Ye fearful saints, fresh courage take,
The clouds ye so much dread
Are big with mercy, and shall break
In blessings on your head.

Judge not the Lord by feeble sense,
But trust him for his grace;

Behind a frowning providence
He hides a smiling face.

His purposes will ripen fast,
Unfolding every hour;
The bud may have a bitter taste,
But sweet will be the flower.

Blind unbelief is sure to err,
And scan his work in vain;
God is his own interpreter,
And he will make it plain.

Words: William Cowper (1731–1800)
Music: LONDON NEW. Melody from the Scottish Psalter (1635)
The feast of St. Nicholas (Santa Claus) is celebrated today.

Every child has heard of Santa Claus, and knows exactly what he does! But not everyone knows the truth behind the legends of the saintly man who was Bishop of Myra in the early fourth century. The English composer Benjamin Britten (1913–76) took the story of life of St. Nicholas and made it into a choral work in 1948. In that work, there are congregational hymns too, and "God moves in a mysterious way" comes at the very end, as everyone joins together to praise God for his many gifts in creation. And of course, one of the great gifts that God gives us are the saints, those men and women of courage, conviction, and faith who inspire, lead, and teach us, long after they have died.

By the sixth century, Nicholas had aroused a certain following, and in the ninth century Methodius of Constantinople articulated some of the legends that had sprung up about his life and works. By the thirteenth century, when Jacobus de Voragine collected together his legends of the saints known as *The Golden Legend*, Nicholas' reputation was firmly established. By the late nineteenth century, St. Nicholas' name had evolved into Santa Claus via the Dutch version of his name, Sinter Klaas, and he became a figure of great interest. Connecting all the legends together was a recurring theme—of Nicholas' special patronage of sailors and of children.

Whether we celebrate the feast of St. Nicholas or not, there can be no doubt that he existed, even if some of the legends about him are quite elaborate. In one sense, we must say that Father Christmas exists.

The difficulty today comes when Santa Claus (Father Christmas) is confused with Jesus, such that many agonize over whether or not to tell their children about Santa Claus bringing presents. Children write to him, and a whole industry has arisen around the plastic patron saint of present-giving. If Santa Claus and Jesus are too much associated, then there really is the risk that when children realize that Santa Claus is a modern commodity, they will throw the baby Jesus out with the bathwater-loving saint. A recent advertising campaign even portrayed Santa Claus in the manger, as a way of emphasizing the confusion that currently exists. "Go on, ask him for something" read the caption. In that image lies the fundamental truth and purpose about Nicholas, for he, as a saint, would never have wanted the attention on himself but would have always desired to witness to Christ, his Lord and Savior. Santa Claus witnesses to Christ, and we must never forget that.

Prayer

O God, the Father of Christmas, and of all time, send us your Holy Spirit, that we may be brought the gifts of love, joy, and peace that you desire for your children in this and every age, for the sake of your Son, Jesus Christ our Lord. Amen.

Blessed be the Lord God of Israel,
for he has looked favorably on his people and redeemed them.
He has raised up a mighty savior for us
in the house of his servant David,
as he spoke through the mouth of his holy prophets from of old,
that we would be saved from our enemies
and from the hand of all who hate us.
Thus he has shown the mercy promised to our ancestors,
and has remembered his holy covenant,
the oath that he swore to our ancestor Abraham,
to grant us that we, being rescued
from the hands of our enemies,
might serve him without fear, in holiness and righteousness
before him all our days.
And you, child, will be called the prophet of the Most High;
for you will go before the Lord to prepare his ways,
to give knowledge of salvation to his people
by the forgiveness of their sins.
By the tender mercy of our God,
the dawn from on high will break upon us,
to give light to those who sit in darkness
and in the shadow of death,
to guide our feet into the way of peace.
—Luke 1:68–79

This is the record of John, when the Jews sent priests and Levites from Jerusalem to ask him, Who art thou?
And he confessed, and denied not; and said plainly, I am not the Christ.

And they asked him, What art thou then? Art thou Elias? And he
said, I am not. Art thou the prophet? And he answered, No.
Then said they unto him, What art thou? that we may give an
answer unto them that sent us. What sayest thou of thyself?
And he said, I am the voice of him that cryeth in the wilderness,
Make straight the way of the Lord.

Words: John 1:19–23 (based on King James Bible)
Music: Orlando Gibbons (1583–1625)

There are several paintings by the Italian Renaissance painter
Raphael (1483–1520) depicting John the Baptist and Jesus
together as babies. One of them, known as the Alba Madonna,
is a round painting, about three feet in diameter, housed in the
National Gallery of Art in Washington DC. Recently restored, it
is beautiful in every sense of the word, with rich blues, greens,
and pinks used to depict Mary's clothes, the grass, and the flesh
tones of the two children.

In the picture we see Mary humbly seated on the ground against
a rural background, reaching out with one hand to steady the two
boys, her other hand clasping a Bible, with her finger placed
between two pages as if to preserve the page that she is reading.
John the Baptist and Jesus are portrayed as though playing together.
In John's hand is a little staff, but very clearly at the top we can see
a cross-piece, indicating that even at birth there is an overshadowing
of the pain and suffering that will emerge when these two little boys
are grown up. Although John is holding the little cross up for Jesus,
Jesus himself is seen to be grasping it, as though receiving it from
his slightly older relative. Nearby, anemones are growing, classically
symbolic of Mary's sorrow over the suffering of Christ.

John's cross may be a little one compared to Christ's, but he too will suffer and die, a martyr in the cause of free speech (see Matthew 14:1–13). In another Raphael painting, the Madonna and Child with the Infant Baptist, we see the same characters, and a similar staff with a cross. This time, however, it is not the cross that the baby Christ grasps, but a red carnation, symbolizing the pure love that will be expressed by his death.

It is clear from these pictures and from the Gospels that John and Jesus had an interesting and possibly close relationship. Their mothers are related (Luke 1:36), and Mary visits Elizabeth when pregnant (Luke 1:39–45). When Herod eventually kills John in a fit of weakness and false integrity, Jesus is described as withdrawing to a deserted place by himself, presumably to grieve (Matthew 14:13). Luke begins his Gospel with an account of how Zechariah, John's father, is told by the angel Gabriel that in spite of all evidence to the contrary, he and his wife Elizabeth will have a child—a very special, Spirit-filled child who will turn people to God, bringing much joy and preparing the way of the Lord (Luke 1:13–17). Zechariah's response is one of disbelief, and this provokes Gabriel to punish him with silence throughout the pregnancy. When eventually John is born, Zechariah is able to speak again. He names the child "John," as Gabriel instructed him, and then utters a prophecy that is known to the church as the Benedictus, from the Latin for its opening words (Luke 1:68–79).

When Archbishop Thomas Cranmer created the Book of Common Prayer in 1549, he continued the tradition of using Luke 1:68–79 as a canticle, to be said after the second lesson at Morning Prayer. Thus Zechariah's prophecy has become part of the spiritual lifeblood of the church. His words glow with

Advent's expectancy of light: during this season we anticipate the blaze of illumination coming into the world with which the other John opens his Gospel. He reminds us that his namesake, the Baptist, is not the light, and proceeds immediately to recount the story by which John the Baptist is heard specifically to proclaim the coming of the Messiah and to deny that it is himself.

Orlando Gibbons was one of the greatest English composers of the seventeenth century, and this setting of a passage from John's Gospel is one of his most famous works. When Gibbons was 21, King James I offered him the post of organist of the Chapel Royal in London, where he remained until his death at the age of 41.

His setting of John 1:19–23 is a distinctive and exquisite piece, which conveys in musical terms the curt and discourteous approach to John by the religious leaders of his day, demanding to know who he is and what is his business. John had been baptizing in the wilderness, and was causing quite a stir by calling sinners to repentance in preparation for the coming of the Messiah. This music is not the equivalent of Renaissance painting, where almost every brushstroke is loaded with symbolism; rather, Gibbons' approach lets the English text speak clearly, such that we do not need symbols or allegorical images to understand the significance of what is going on. Yet both Raphael and Gibbons have a clear sense of the significance of John as forerunner of Christ, "making straight" the way of the Lord (Isaiah 40:3), for it is a way that leads through death and resurrection to redemption. And it is the way on which we are all called to walk, whether we live in sixteenth-century Italy, Elizabethan England, or the Internet-ready twenty-first-century global community.

Prayer

Tender, merciful God, who sent your Son Jesus to be the hope of the world, give light to all who sit in darkness and the shadow of death, that all your people may serve you without fear and be guided into the way of peace, which he illuminates this very day. Amen.

"Be dressed for action and have your lamps lit; be like those who are
waiting for their master to return from the wedding banquet, so that
they may open the door for him as soon as he comes and knocks.
Blessed are those slaves whom the master finds alert when he comes;
truly I tell you, he will fasten his belt and have them sit down to eat,
and he will come and serve them. If he comes during the middle of the
night, or near dawn, and finds them so, blessed are those slaves."
—Luke 12:35–38

Thou whose almighty word
Chaos and darkness heard,
And took their flight;
Hear us, we humbly pray,
And where the gospel day
Sheds not its glorious ray
Let there be light.

Thou who didst come to bring
On thy redeeming wing
Healing and sight,
Health to the sick in mind,
Sight to the inly blind,
O now to all mankind
Let there be light.

Spirit of truth and love,
Life-giving, holy Dove,
Speed forth thy flight;
Move o'er the waters' face,

Bearing the lamp of grace,
And in earth's darkest place
Let there be light.

Blessed and holy Three,
Glorious Trinity,
Wisdom, Love, Might,
Boundless as ocean's tide
Rolling in fullest pride,
Through the world far and wide
Let there be light.

Words: John Marriott (1780–1825)
Music: MOSCOW, adapted from Felice Giardini (1716–96)

Advent is a dark time of year. The Christmas lights may well be up early, but before Christmas Day dawns they serve to emphasize the darkness in which they shine. In the northern hemisphere, the nights are longest at this time of year, and this can affect us in many ways. Some people suffer from a recently recognized condition known as Seasonal Affective Disorder (SAD), which causes a kind of depression brought about by the lack of sunlight. Our bodies and our minds react to, and need, light.

As well as being physically dark, Advent can also be emotionally or spiritually dark. As Christmas approaches, we might be reminded of lost loved ones or of past sadnesses. The lack of light at this time of the year seems to promote reflection on times past and fading memories. In the winter months, some people do not go out at night because they are fearful to walk the streets, and therefore feel more trapped at home at this time of year, as the days are short.

Advent, perhaps more than any other season, can expose brokenness in our lives and world. It is not so much a time to be bleak, but a time to examine the world around us and become aware of the poverty and pain in which so many live. Sometimes it may feel that we have been struck by a ray of darkness, piercing complacency and comfort and destroying security. Even if we reflect on the second coming, we are up against a hope that has so far not materialized. The early church believed in an imminent return of Christ, yet we continue to wait. The master, it seems, has been delayed in his arrival.

Our hope and desire, as Christians, must ultimately be that the light of God will shine in the dark places of sin and despair. We experience this when we place our trust in God and are led away from the darkness of pain to the healing power of Christ's light. It is this desire that prompted John Marriott to write his now-famous hymn. It is thoroughly trinitarian: each of the first three verses takes in turn Father, Son, and Holy Spirit, and the fourth is a doxology, praising all three in one. Shining through it is the creative, sustaining, and healing light of God.

It can be very tempting to dwell unduly upon events and feelings that upset us. Nevertheless, comfort is at hand through the ministry of friends and fellow Christians, in whom God's healing Spirit is at work. Through the encounter between light and darkness, sorrow and joy, we may experience an authentic Advent, in which gloom and sorrow are alleviated by a positive hope in the return of Christ to make all things new. Giardini's tune combined with Marriott's words make for a rousing hymn. Singing it in the darkness can help us to remember not only God's light of creation, but also the light of Christ coming into the world, to illuminate, cleanse, and heal.

Prayer

O God and Father of all light, look down on your expectant people and give us your hope and your joy, that as we wait upon your promises we may be bathed in the light of your love, until that day when you return in glory to make all things new and good and true in your Son, Jesus Christ our Lord. Amen.

December 9   Earth was waiting, spent and restless

I consider that the sufferings of this present time are not worth comparing with the glory about to be revealed to us. For the creation waits with eager longing for the revealing of the children of God; for the creation was subjected to futility, not of its own will but by the will of the one who subjected it, in hope that the creation itself will be set free from its bondage to decay and will obtain the freedom of the glory of the children of God. We know that the whole creation has been groaning in labor pains until now; and not only the creation, but we ourselves, who have the first fruits of the Spirit, groan inwardly while we wait for adoption, the redemption of our bodies. For in hope we were saved. Now hope that is seen is not hope. For who hopes for what is seen? But if we hope for what we do not see, we wait for it with patience.
—Romans 8:18–25

Earth was waiting, spent and restless,
with a mingled hope and fear,
faithful men and women praying,
  "Surely, Lord, the day is near:
the Desire of all the nations—
it is time he should appear!"

Then the Spirit of the Highest
to a Virgin meek came down,
and he burdened her with blessing,
and he pained her with renown;
for she bore the Lord's Anointed
for his cross and for his crown.

Earth has groaned and labored for him
since the ages first began,
for in him was hid the secret
which through all the ages ran—
Son of Mary, Son of David,
Son of God, and Son of Man.

Words: Walter Chalmers Smith (1824–1908)
Music: PICARDY. French carol found in Tiersot's Mélodies, Paris, 1887

Advent is, most of all, a time of waiting—waiting on the Lord, and waiting for the Lord—except that perhaps we have forgotten how to wait. For twenty-first-century humanity, waiting takes up the space between a desire and a result. We do not want or expect that waiting space to be very big, even though waiting can occupy a significant portion of our lives. We have to wait for things—things we want, things we need, and things we dread. We are not in control of our lives as we might want to be, or as we might suppose ourselves to be. We can fly, speak across oceans and access vast amounts of information, but we cannot prevent our deaths, reverse time, or predict the future.

The words of this relatively recent carol reflect today's mood very well. "Earth was waiting, spent and restless" is a phrase that might apply to an individual, worn out with personal frustrations, or it could apply to the whole world, groaning with exhaustion after a catalog of natural disasters, shaking, flooding, or starving the populations of various corners of the globe. The apostle Paul's references to futility and the bondage of decay are dark words, which seem so apposite when we turn on the television news.

How are we to handle our restlessness, our fear, doubt, or despair? So often, our response to frustration or impatience is fatalism: if we cannot control our lives, then we merely accept what is thrown at us, for it is all "meant to be." Such an approach is hardly more helpful than the manic desire to control everything and everyone, for fatalism more or less denies us a place in the world, and can lead to a certain abandonment of personal responsibility in actions, relationships, or desires. This may well be a problem for our age, in which fatalism and freedom have merged in a society that is both fascinated and appalled by conventional faith.

But Advent is not merely about waiting; it is about hopeful waiting. We wait for our Lord of all hopefulness, praying that the darkness of life today can be illuminated by God's light, burned away in the glow of his love revealed in the redeeming work of Jesus Christ. When we read the passage from Romans carefully, and heed the words of this hymn, we realize that our waiting may not be pleasant. Our purpose on earth in the intervening time is not simply to be entertained in some kind of antechamber to heavenly bliss.

For Walter Smith, the solution to doom and gloom is to be found in Christ, the immortal, invisible light, supremely human, supremely divine, through whom the redemption of the whole creation becomes possible.

The old French tune PICARDY, which fits so well with Smith's words, is more often associated with the ancient hymn "Let all mortal flesh keep silence." That eucharistic hymn has a seasonal flavor too, and the sense of reverence conveyed by a slow rendition of the tune can equally reflect the mysteriousness of the incarnation. For some, the thought of an end time when creation's groaning will cease and Christ will return is something rather terrifying, while for others it is something eagerly anticipated. The thought of the glory of God revealed in a second coming of Christ is truly an amazing one, which we can hardly comprehend, although it may not be so hard to welcome the idea that the pain of the world can be likened to labor pains, excruciating to bear but necessary for a wonderful, exciting, and new creation.

Prayer

O Jesus, Son of Mary, Son of David, bless us when we feel burdened with the cares of the world or pained by the hurts of others, that we may be refreshed by the mystery of your presence among us, and inspired by the renown of your cross-crowning love, for you are Son of God, and Son of Man, then, now, and for ever. Amen.

December 10 **People, look East**

Arise, shine; for your light has come, and the glory of the Lord has risen upon you. For darkness shall cover the earth, and thick darkness the peoples; but the Lord will arise upon you, and his glory will appear over you. Nations shall come to your light, and kings to the brightness of your dawn. Lift up your eyes and look around; they all gather together, they come to you; your sons shall come from far away, and your daughters shall be carried on their nurses' arms. Then you shall see and be radiant; your heart shall thrill and rejoice, because the abundance of the sea shall be brought to you, the wealth of the nations shall come to you.

—Isaiah 60:1–5

People, look East, the time is near
of the crowning of the year.
Make your house fair as you are able,
trim the hearth, and set the table.
People, look East, and sing today:
Love the Guest is on the way.

Furrows, be glad, though earth is bare,
one more seed is planted there:
Give up your strength the seed to nourish,
that in course the flower may flourish.
People, look East, and sing today:
Love the Rose is on the way.

Stars, keep the watch, when night is dim
one more light the bowl shall brim.
Shining beyond the frosty weather,
bright as sun and moon together.

People, look East, and sing today:
Love the Star is on the way.
Angels, announce to man and beast
Him who cometh from the East.
Set ev'ry peak and valley humming
with the word, the Lord is coming.
People, look East, and sing today:
Love the Lord is on the way.

Words: Eleanor Farjeon (1881–1965) © Oxford University Press.
Music: Seventeenth century or earlier

The English writer Eleanor Farjeon may be best remembered as the author of the hymn "Morning has broken," but she also wrote collections of stories, plays based on fairy tales, poetry, and other books. She also wrote novels, as well as plays, poetry, and biographical works, and she was a friend of D. H. Lawrence and Walter de la Mare.

Her Advent carol "People, look East," draws its title from a passage in the Apocryphal book of Baruch:

Arise, O Jerusalem, stand upon the height; look toward the east, and see your children gathered from west and east at the word of the Holy One, rejoicing that God has remembered them. For they went out from you on foot, led away by their enemies; but God will bring them back to you, carried in glory, as on a royal throne.
—Baruch 5:5–7

Baruch was Jeremiah's secretary (see Jeremiah 32:12–16), but it is unlikely that he actually wrote the book that bears his name. Nevertheless, Baruch is written from the perspective of dispersed

Jews, and contains a wonderful passage that looks both forward and eastward to salvation. Baruch's readers are literally looking eastward to Jerusalem, their homeland, from which they have been exiled. Nowadays we might recall that the sun rises in the east, and thus it is in that direction that we look for the rising of Christ—the advent of the sun of righteousness. Isaiah writes in a similar vein in that most evocative passage, "Arise, shine; for your light has come." He also tells his people to look eastward to the rising of the sun, and proclaims a time when those far away will return at the dawn of a new age of prosperity and joy, replacing the sufferings of exile.

Eleanor Farjeon's spiritual journey was a long one, which culminated with her becoming a Roman Catholic at the age of 70. "People, look East" was one of six carols that she wrote for her friend Percy Dearmer's groundbreaking *The Oxford Book of Carols*, published in 1928. The words are striking, and are reminiscent of the Benedicite, a canticle that is often substituted for the Te Deum at Morning Prayer during Advent and Lent. (A canticle is a biblical text or collection of verses arranged for singing or chanting.) Its text comes from the "Song of the Three," which is the apocryphal prayer of thanksgiving offered by Shadrach, Meshach, and Abednego when they remained unhurt upon being cast into the fiery furnace for refusing to worship King Nebuchadnezzar's golden statue.

There is a similar "earthy" theme in Farjeon's words, which seem to combine the feel of winter "good cheer" with a biblical resonance and theological purpose. This theology is expressed in the last line of each verse: "Love," personified in Christ, is the guest, the rose, the star, and the Lord. In this imagery we are reminded that Christ comes among us, as one of us but also as a kind of stranger, a guest, whom we must welcome—and we must prepare to welcome him into our homes and our hearts.

Prayer

Father God, you greet us in Christ by his birth among us, and by your Holy Spirit you continue to offer your saving love to every corner of the world. As we send seasonal greetings to those whom we love and care for, hear the unspoken prayers of our hearts, and bless all those to whom we write, whether they be near or far. Amen.

December 11   Born in the night

And he will come to Zion as Redeemer, to those in Jacob who turn from transgression, says the Lord. And as for me, this is my covenant with them, says the Lord: my spirit that is upon you, and my words that I have put in your mouth, shall not depart out of your mouth, or out of the mouths of your children, or out of the mouths of your children's children, says the Lord, from now on and forever.

Arise, shine; for your light has come, and the glory of the Lord has risen upon you. For darkness shall cover the earth, and thick darkness the peoples; but the Lord will arise upon you, and his glory will appear over you. Nations shall come to your light, and kings to the brightness of your dawn. Lift up your eyes and look around; they all gather together, they come to you; your sons shall come from far away, and your daughters shall be carried on their nurses' arms. Then you shall see and be radiant; your heart shall thrill and rejoice, because the abundance of the sea shall be brought to you, the wealth of the nations shall come to you. —Isaiah 59:20–60:5

Born in the night,
     Mary's child.
A long way from your home;
Coming in need,
     Mary's child,
Born in a borrowed room.

Clear shining light,
     Mary's child,
Your face lights up our way;
Light of the world,
     Mary's child,
Dawn on our darkened day.

Truth of our life,
>Mary's child,
You tell us God is good;
Prove it is true,
>Mary's child,
Go to your cross of wood.

Hope of the world,
>Mary's child,
You're coming soon to reign;
King of the earth,
>Mary's child,
Walk in our streets again.

Words and music: Geoffrey Ainger (b. 1925) © Stainer and Bell

Among the hundreds of Advent and Christmas carols that are available to us to sing, meditate upon, pray through, and worship with, this one is distinctive because it is addressed to Jesus. Very few of the carols that English-speakers love to sing are actually addressed to Jesus, or even to God, although there are the more sentimental kind, addressed as rocking carols to an idealized baby Jesus, as in "The rocking carol" and the second half of "Away in a manger":
. . . I love thee, Lord Jesus! Look down from the sky,
And stay by my bedside till morning is nigh.
Be near me, Lord Jesus; I ask thee to stay
Close by me for ever, and love me, I pray.
Bless all the dear children in thy tender care,
And fit us for heaven, to live with thee there.

Meanwhile, we are happy to address ourselves and each other in most of the hymns and carols we sing. Many are a rallying cry to offer praise, to "come and worship," and they often do this by re-telling the story of the incarnation. Some carols—strangely, perhaps—are addressed to slaughtered children ("The Coventry Carol"); to the Christmas tree ("O Tannenbaum"); to Mary ("Mary, blessed teenage mother"); to Jesus' birthplace ("Bethlehem of noblest cities" and "O little town of Bethlehem"); or to angels ("Angels from the realms of glory"). Other carols are narrative, even dramatic in form ("Good King Wenceslas" and "We three kings").

With "Born in the night," however, we can rejoice in a set of words that unashamedly form a prayer to Jesus. And what a lovely carol this is: the words are powerful, and the tune (MARY'S CHILD) is delightful. Put together, they contrast profoundly, for words and music bring out and emphasize the joy and the pain which spell out the irony of Christmas. Here in words and music is a carol that warms our hearts with the good news, sounding a bit like a lilting lullaby, but that also cuts us to the quick with its honesty about the circumstances of Christ's birth, the darkness of the world, the crucifixion, and the second coming.

At first glance, it may appear that Geoffrey Ainger is telling us that Jesus was born in the middle of the night. Many people believe that he was, of course: the angels appear to the shepherds by night, and the wise men follow a star, all of which lures us into the Christmas card image of a night-time birth in a nice clean stable, under a clear midnight sky. Perhaps Mary was in labor for part of a night (many mothers are!), but this romanticized vision is not directly drawn from Scripture, and we might even note that the shepherds were told that "this day" a child has been born (Luke 2:11). The "night" of the carol is not simply a reference to the popular assumption that Jesus was born in the hours of darkness, but it is a metaphorical night: the night-time of the world, a dark time in which Christ, light of the world, appears. We may not be sure of the literal truth of Christ's being "born in the night," but references to the "cross of wood" remind us of its truth in spiritual terms. Christ came, as in the words of Isaiah's prophecy, to a people who "walked in darkness" (Isaiah 9:2).

Yet wherever there is darkness there is hope of light. The world is in need of salvation, and each one of us needs a Savior. Wherever anyone walks in need or suffering, the light of Christ, who is the hope of the world, can break through. The reality of distress in our world is obvious, and many live without hope. But we do find hope in the conclusion of this carol—the hope of the world, the hoped-for return of Christ, which forms the theme of Advent.

Prayer
Mary's child Jesus, hope of the world, light up the way of faith for all who walk in doubt, loneliness, need, or darkness. As you are goodness and truth in human form, grant us to borrow from you some splinters of your compassion, that in our small way we may anticipate the coming of your kingdom here on this fragile earth, for you are coming to reign, in the name of the Father and in the power of the Spirit. Amen.

The next day he saw Jesus coming towards him and declared, "Here is the Lamb of God who takes away the sin of the world! This is he of whom I said, 'After me comes a man who ranks ahead of me because he was before me.' I myself did not know him; but I came baptizing with water for this reason, that he might be revealed to Israel." And John testified, "I saw the Spirit descending from heaven like a dove, and it remained on him. I myself did not know him, but the one who sent me to baptize with water said to me, 'He on whom you see the Spirit descend and remain is the one who baptizes with the Holy Spirit.' And I myself have seen and have testified that this is the Son of God." The next day John again was standing with two of his disciples, and as he watched Jesus walk by, he exclaimed, "Look, here is the Lamb of God!" The two disciples heard him say this, and they followed Jesus.

—John 1:29–37

Little Lamb, who made thee?
Dost thou know who made thee?
Gave thee life, and bid thee feed
By the stream and o'er the mead;
Gave thee clothing of delight,
Softest clothing, woolly, bright;
Gave thee such a tender voice,
Making all the vales rejoice?
Little Lamb, who made thee?
Dost thou know who made thee?

Little Lamb, I'll tell thee,
Little Lamb, I'll tell thee:

He is called by thy name,
For he calls himself a Lamb.
He is meek, and he is mild;
He became a little child.
I a child, and thou a lamb.
We are called by his name.
Little Lamb, God bless thee!
Little Lamb, God bless thee!

Words: William Blake (1757–1827)
Music: John Tavener (b. 1934)

The significance of sheep is well attested in the Bible. According to my computer, there are 189 references to sheep in the New Revised Standard Version of the Bible, and if you add in words like "ewe" and "ram," you get over 700 references. The most important biblical story about sheep is, of course, the one that precedes the final flight from Egypt, when the angel of death "passes over" the Israelites, striking down the firstborn of the Egyptians. The people of God are instructed to kill a lamb, smear its blood on the doorway as a sign of allegiance to God, and to eat the flesh, hastily, in readiness for flight (Exodus 12). The Passover is a continuing memorial of that ancient and significant event.

Sheep were incredibly useful animals and were easily domesticated. As such they were immensely valuable and had to be looked after and guarded. King David, we know, was not only a good musician and giant killer, but he started his career as a shepherd, keeping predators away from the flock at night. The shepherds in the story of Jesus' birth were doing much the same. At night, the shepherd would bring the animals safely into a cave or some other fold, and would sleep across the entrance to protect them, literally "laying down his life" for them.

By the time we reach the Gospels, we have stories of lost sheep and a good shepherd, but also the famous statement from John the Baptist, who identifies Jesus as the Lamb of God (John 1:36). New Testament theology associates Jesus with that first lamb of God, the Passover lamb of Exodus 12, and in John's Gospel the crucifixion is described as taking place while the Passover lambs were being slaughtered in readiness for the festival the following day (John 19:14–16). Easter and Passover are inextricably and symbolically linked, as are Passover and eucharist.

But Jesus is not only associated with the sacrificial lamb, whose blood is spilled so that his people may be saved. Jesus is also the good shepherd, the carer, the shepherd of our souls. The prophet Ezekiel foresaw this when he wrote, "For thus says the Lord God: I myself will search for my sheep, and will seek them out. As shepherds seek out their flocks when they are among their scattered sheep, so I will seek out my sheep" (Ezekiel 34:11–12).

William Blake played on this overlap of sheep and shepherd in his delightful children's poem "The Lamb," which was part of his collection *Songs of Innocence*, written in 1789. He added *Songs of Experience* in 1794, creating a double set of poetry that underlined the tragic but truthful discrepancy in life between the world of pastoral innocence and the cynical, repressed world of adulthood. So we have the apparent meekness of "The Lamb," which contrasts with "The Tyger" in Songs of Experience ("Tyger, tyger, burning bright! . . .did he who made the lamb, make thee?").

Both these poems have been set to music by the contemporary composer John Tavener, and "The Lamb," composed in 1982, has become a favorite for unaccompanied choir. It is quite a simple piece, but contains within itself a harmonic ambiguity. We are transported to Blake's innocent world of childhood, but as the music drifts in its haunting way, we are never quite allowed to become submerged in a safe soundworld. There are melancholic undertones that speak of the tragedy of lost innocence, of the fact that the little lamb will not live long; that the cute animal beloved of little children has the same creator as you and I. It is an unusual Christmas carol and, like most, is popular because it sounds nice and has sentimental words. But listen to the music carefully and study the words, and there is darkness within—the darkness of future pain and of betrayal. The innocence of the Christ-child will be betrayed and the roles reversed as we become the children, the children of God, and Jesus the lamb, sacrificed once and for all upon the cross.

Prayer

Salvation belongs to you, our God who is seated on the throne, and to the Lamb! As we remember that your Son was born innocent of all sin, but chose to taint himself with the sin of the world, help us always to praise you: blessing and glory and wisdom and thanksgiving and honor and power and might be to you for ever and ever! Amen.

December 13 Santa Lucia

"You are the light of the world. A city built on a hill cannot be hidden. No one after lighting a lamp puts it under the bushel basket, but on the lampstand, and it gives light to all in the house. In the same way, let your light shine before others, so that they may see your good works and give glory to your Father in heaven."
—Matthew 5:14–16

Hark! through the darksome night
Sounds come a winging:
Lo! 'tis the Queen of Light
Joyfully singing.
Clad in her garment white,
Wearing her crown of light,
Santa Lucia, Santa Lucia.

Deep in the northern sky
Bright stars are beaming;
Christmas is drawing nigh,
Candles are gleaming.
Welcome you vision rare,
Lights glowing in your hair.
Santa Lucia, Santa Lucia.

The darkness shall soon depart
from the earth's valleys
thus she speaks
a wonderful word to us
The day shall rise anew
from the rosy sky.
Santa Lucia, Santa Lucia.

Words and Music: Traditional (translation compiled from various sources)

Today is the feast day of St. Lucy, patron saint of the blind. According to various legends and sources, she was martyred in 304 in Syracuse, Sicily. She is still revered as the patron saint of that city (although her body is now said to lie in Venice), and she is associated with light because it was said that she used to visit Christians who were in hiding in dark underground tunnels. To light the way she wore a wreath of candles on her head.

Apparently her family was wealthy, but her father died young, leaving her in the care of her widowed mother, who intended her to marry a pagan called Paschiasus. Lucy preferred to remain unmarried and went to pray at the tomb of St. Agatha, which was in Catania, also in Sicily. Consequently, her mother was cured of a long illness, and became more amenable to her daughter's request not to marry but instead to give her wealth to the poor and commit her life to God. Her suitor was less impressed, though, and denounced her to the Roman authorities. They determined that she should be sent to a brothel, but Lucy refused and they could not enforce the ruling. According to legend, she plucked out her own eyes and sent them to Paschiasus on a plate, which is why she is often portrayed in art as carrying a dish containing her eyes. (Other legends say that her eyes were put out by her persecutors.) Then she was condemned to be burnt alive, but she proved to be impervious to the flames, so she was finally killed by the sword.

All this is likely to have taken place during the reign of Emperor Diocletian (284–305), who instigated a particularly severe persecution in 303. Nowadays, Lucy is still revered in Scandinavia. For this day, each village elects its own Lucia (or Lucy), and this "Lucia Queen," wearing a crown of lit candles, leads children singing traditional carols in a procession through the home or in the streets. In Stockholm each year, the "Lucia Queen" is crowned by the winner of the Nobel Prize for Literature. Lucia's Day symbolically opens the Christmas celebrations in Scandinavia, bringing hope and light during the darkest months of the year, for far into the northern hemisphere there are days with no sunlight at all for part of the year. Before the reform of the Gregorian calendar in the sixteenth century, Lucy's Day fell on the winter solstice (now December 21), the shortest day.

The feast of St. Lucy ("Santa Lucia") is now celebrated as a festival of light, and it has spread to churches all over the world, as Santa Lucia is celebrated with a blend of Christmas carols, processions, preaching, and ritual. At the heart of the service is the Santa Lucia procession, headed by a girl wearing a crown of candles and escorted by other young people as she brings in the light. All are dressed in white, bearing candles and singing, and the boys wear traditional white cone-shaped hats. We might think of Christ, the light of the world, born in a dark stable to bring light and life, or we might think of the ancient festivals of light that marked the turning of the globe, hailing the beginning of the end of the long nights, and the return of the sun.

Prayer

O Lord, the light of whose love shines in the world, accept our praises and prayers, that, illuminated by you, we may always offer worship worthy of your glory, until that day when we, with all who are clothed in white, shall sit at your feet in the heavenly kingdom, where you reign, king of light and truth, with the Father and Holy Spirit, ever one God, now and for ever. Amen.

Of the Father's heart begotten

An account of the genealogy of Jesus the Messiah, the son of David, the son of Abraham. Abraham was the father of Isaac, and Isaac the father of Jacob, and Jacob the father of Judah and his brothers, and Judah the father of Perez and Zerah by Tamar, and Perez the father of Hezron, and Hezron the father of Aram, and Aram the father of Aminadab, and Aminadab the father of Nahshon, and Nahshon the father of Salmon, and Salmon the father of Boaz by Rahab, and Boaz the father of Obed by Ruth, and Obed the father of Jesse, and Jesse the father of King David.

And David was the father of Solomon by the wife of Uriah, and Solomon the father of Rehoboam, and Rehoboam the father of Abijah, and Abijah the father of Asaph, and Asaph the father of Jehoshaphat, and Jehoshaphat the father of Joram, and Joram the father of Uzziah, and Uzziah the father of Jotham, and Jotham the father of Ahaz, and Ahaz the father of Hezekiah, and Hezekiah the father of Manasseh, and Manasseh the father of Amos, and Amos the father of Josiah, and Josiah the father of Jechoniah and his brothers, at the time of the deportation to Babylon.

And after the deportation to Babylon: Jechoniah was the father of Salathiel, and Salathiel the father of Zerubbabel, and Zerubbabel the father of Abiud, and Abiud the father of Eliakim, and Eliakim the father of Azor, and Azor the father of Zadok, and Zadok the father of Achim, and Achim the father of Eliud, and Eliud the father of Eleazar, and Eleazar the father of Matthan, and Matthan the father of Jacob, and Jacob the father of Joseph the husband of Mary, of whom Jesus was born, who is called the Messiah.

So all the generations from Abraham to David are fourteen generations;
and from David to the deportation to Babylon, fourteen generations; and
from the deportation to Babylon to the Messiah, fourteen generations.
—Matthew 1:1–17

Of the Father's heart begotten,
Ere the world from chaos rose,
He is Alpha: from that Fountain
All that is and hath been flows;
He is Omega, of all things
Yet to come the mystic Close,
Evermore and evermore.

O how blest that wondrous birthday,
When the Maid the curse retrieved,
Brought to birth mankind's salvation,
By the Holy Ghost conceived;
And the Babe, the world's Redeemer,
In her loving arms received,
Evermore and evermore.

This is he, whom seer and sibyl
Sang in ages long gone by;
This is he of old revealed
In the page of prophecy;
Lo! he comes the promised Savior;
Let the world his praises cry!
Evermore and evermore.

Let the storm and summer sunshine,
Gliding stream and sounding shore,
Sea and forest, frost and zephyr,
Day and night their Lord adore;
Let creation join to laud thee
Through the ages evermore,
Evermore and evermore.

Sing, ye heights of heaven, his praises;
Angels and Archangels, sing!
Wheresoe'er ye be, ye faithful,
Let your joyous anthems ring,
Every tongue his name confessing,
Countless voices answering
Evermore and evermore.

Words: Latin, by Prudentius, trans. Roby Furley Davis (1866–1937)
Music: DIVINUM MYSTERIUM. Melody from Piae Cantiones,
Theoderici Petri Nylandensis, 1582

At the very beginning of Matthew's Gospel we find what the
NRSV calls "the genealogy of Jesus the Messiah."
Matthew wants to remind us that Jesus had a significant birth-
line, through Joseph, the husband of his mother. It seems like just
a list of names, and is often ignored. But in these names, some
obscure, some familiar, we see people whose role in the history of
salvation was immensely significant, and others who are hardly
remembered today. Matthew's list is a golden thread of spiritual
greatness, sewing together the greatest lineage ever recorded. He
knew his heritage well, and, in writing for those who had a sense

of their place in history, he draws Jesus' family tree in great detail. His readers knew these figures better than we do now, and would have been suitably impressed by the connections he makes. That Jesus was directly descended from Abraham and David was of great importance to the Jews whom Matthew was evangelizing.

$$\wr \quad \wr \quad \wr$$

It is not only about who you know, but what you know. In that thread lie strands of wisdom, passed from one generation to another. Just as musicians like to trace their musical education back to a great composer or virtuoso, religious leaders sometimes boast of their mentors, having learned from widely respected elders. Jesus, therefore, is presented as sitting at the feet of a revered line of religious leaders. So it is not just who his earthly ancestors were that matters, but the fact that they were also his spiritual fathers. For then it adds up and points us towards a recognition of who his heavenly Father was, and is, and ever shall be.

We should not be surprised that there is sin in this list. There is sin everywhere, even among those whom we revere as great religious leaders. This may be a list of spiritual heroes, with whom Matthew wants to associate Jesus, but as saints they are also sinners. David, infamously, committed adultery with Bathsheba, the wife of Uriah the Hittite, whom David caused to be killed in battle; and his son Solomon, although blessed with wisdom, was not without his faults. Solomon's son Rehoboam also forsook the law of the Lord. So it continues, until we reach the man at the head of the list: Jesus. The others, like every human being before or since, were weak and committed sin. Matthew's genealogy carries us through sin until we reach Jesus, who, because he himself is divine and sinless, clears sin away by his death, and turns us all around, pointing us in a new direction and sending us on our way along the road to salvation.

We can see in this list not only a sense of Jesus' place in history, but a sense of the pace of history. Forty-two generations are listed, and Matthew suggests that it was not really very long between Abraham and Christ. Thus Abraham is made real to Jesus' generation, while we need only go back 33 60-year lifetimes to meet Christ. Seen like this, the events of the Bible seem much closer than we might have realized. By reminding his readers of the relatively recent history preceding the birth of Christ, Matthew brings this world nearer in time, and as we read it now, we are reminded that we are closer in time to Matthew than he was to Abraham.

Prayer

Creator God, Father of Jesus from before the world began, your mercy beams from on high like summer sunshine in the dark winter of our hearts. Take the imperfections of our lives and turn them to good, so that we, with all the generations of your children who have gone before us, may find your name on our lips and your love in our hearts, for you reign, Father, Son and Holy Spirit, evermore and evermore. Amen.

This is the truth sent from above

*Then the Lord God formed man from the dust of the ground, and
breathed into his nostrils the breath of life; and the man became a living
being. . . . The Lord God took the man and put him in the garden of
Eden to till it and keep it. And the Lord God commanded the man,
"You may freely eat of every tree of the garden; but of the tree of the
knowledge of good and evil you shall not eat, for in the day that you
eat of it you shall die." Then the Lord God said, "It is not good that
the man should be alone; I will make him a helper as his partner.". . .
So the Lord God caused a deep sleep to fall upon the man, and he
slept; then he took one of his ribs and closed up its place with flesh.
And the rib that the Lord God had taken from the man he made into
a woman and brought her to the man. Then the man said, "This at last
is bone of my bones and flesh of my flesh; this one shall be called
Woman, for out of Man this one was taken." Therefore a man leaves
his father and his mother and clings to his wife, and they become one
flesh. And the man and his wife were both naked, and were not
ashamed.*
—Genesis 2:7, 15–18, 21–25

This is the truth sent from above
The truth of God, the God of love:
Therefore don't turn me from your door
But hearken all, both rich and poor.

The first thing that I do relate
Is that God did man create,
The next thing which to you I'll tell
Woman was made with man to dwell.

And after that, 'twas God's own choice
To place them both in Paradise,
There to remain of evil free,
Except they ate of such a tree.

But they did eat, which was a sin,
And so their ruin did begin,
Ruined themselves, both you and me,
And all of their posterity.

Thus we were heirs to endless woes
Till God and Lord did interpose,
And so a promise soon did run
That He would redeem us by His Son.

And at that season of the year
Our blessed redeemer did appear.
He here did live and here did preach,
And many thousands he did teach.

Thus He in love to us behaved
To show us how we must be saved;
And if you want to know the way,
Be pleased to hear what He did say.

Words and music: English traditional

For many people, this carol will always be associated with the opening section of the *Fantasia on Christmas Carols* written by Ralph Vaughan Williams in 1912. The rather unusual tune was notated by Vaughan Williams, and it has an irregular rhythmic structure, alternating bars of five beats with bars of six. There is no sense of imbalance, however, because it conveys a sense of movement, carrying us forward as the tale unfolds. In this the music complements the long distances in time that the text describes, bringing us from Adam and Eve through to the redeeming work of Jesus.

Vaughan Williams composed the *Fantasia on Christmas Carols* during a period in his life when he had been traveling round Britain, avidly collecting folk music, and it was dedicated to Cecil Sharpe (1859–1924), a fellow folksong collector and friend.

The text of the carol "This is the truth" is all about the history of salvation, taking us right back to the creation of humankind. As in "Adam lay ybounden," which we shall consider tomorrow, we are reminded that the story of Christ was effectively begun at the moment God created the world. A fallen humanity needs a redeemer, and that was the case from the moment that Adam and Eve sinned, resulting in exile from paradise. Consequently, we, the human race, have been "heirs to endless woes," even though there arose a promise that one day we would be redeemed.

♬ ♬ ♬

The promise of redemption comes through Jesus Christ, who is like a second "Adam"— an archetypal human being, who repairs the damage done by his predecessor Adam. God, in Christ, comes and dwells among us, so that by taking on the sin of humanity (begun with and by Adam), he can lift it away from us, as he is lifted up on the Cross. Christ's birth, ministry, passion, and resurrection add up to the great undoing of sin and the re-opening of the way to relationship with the Father. It is this that is the truth, sent down to us by God above. Yet simultaneously, it is the person of Christ, who is the way and the life, who as word-made-flesh, is the truth sent from above.

Prayer

O God of love, who created humanity and placed us in paradise until we were ruined by sin, do not turn us away from your presence, but show us how we must be saved by following in the way of your dear Son Jesus Christ, who was born, lived, and died for us, but who now reigns in glory with you and the Holy Spirit, now and for ever. Amen.

Adam lay ybounden

Now the serpent was more crafty than any other wild animal that the Lord God had made. He said to the woman, "Did God say, 'You shall not eat from any tree in the garden'?" The woman said to the serpent, "We may eat of the fruit of the trees in the garden; but God said, 'You shall not eat of the fruit of the tree that is in the middle of the garden, nor shall you touch it, or you shall die.'" But the serpent said to the woman, "You will not die; for God knows that when you eat of it your eyes will be opened, and you will be like God, knowing good and evil." So when the woman saw that the tree was good for food, and that it was a delight to the eyes, and that the tree was to be desired to make one wise, she took of its fruit and ate; and she also gave some to her husband, who was with her, and he ate. Then the eyes of both were opened, and they knew that they were naked; and they sewed fig leaves together and made loincloths for themselves. They heard the sound of the Lord God walking in the garden at the time of the evening breeze, and the man and his wife hid themselves from the presence of the Lord God among the trees of the garden.

—Genesis 3:1–8

Adam lay ybounden
Bounden in a bond:
Four thousand winter
Thought he not too long.

An all was for an apple,
An apple that he took,
As Clerkes finden
Written in their book.

Ne had the apple taken been,
The apple taken been,
Ne had never our Lady
A been heavene queen.

Blessed be the time
That apple taken was;
Therefore we moun singen:
Deo Gracias!

Words: Fifteenth century
Music: Boris Ord (1897–1961)

S ome of the words in this carol need slight translation into contemporary English: "(y)bounden" means "bound"; "Clerkes" are clerks, or priests; "finden" means "find"; "ne" means something like "not if," and "moun singen" means "must sing." "Deo Gracias" is Latin for "Thanks be to God." The technical term for a carol that uses both Latin and English is "macaronic."

For a Christmas carol, we must notice immediately that Jesus is not mentioned at all. Nevertheless, Christ is implicit throughout. The text is about the sin of Adam and Eve, the eating of the forbidden fruit, which the unknown writer takes to be a happy precursor of the salvation wrought for humankind in and through Christ. The logic is unequivocal: if Adam had not disobeyed God, then humanity would not have fallen into sin; and if that had not happened, we would not have needed redemption. And if we had not needed redemption, there would have been no need for God to send Christ to redeem us, and that means that not only would there have been no crucifixion and resurrection, there would have been no incarnation—no nativity, no

Christmas! The implication is that we would be worse off for having nothing to thank God for. It is almost as if the sin of Adam were a good thing, because it enabled God to do wondrous deeds in Christ; to make Mary the queen of heaven (a Catholic doctrine of the period, still held by many today), and to give us something to sing about.

The reverse logic that we find in this carol does raise some theological conundrums. The apostle Paul famously wrote, "For since death came through a human being, the resurrection of the dead has also come through a human being; for as all die in Adam, so all will be made alive in Christ. But each in his own order: Christ the first fruits, then at his coming those who belong to Christ" (1 Corinthians 15:21–23).

The idea here is that because Adam sinned, humanity was fallen; and Christ, the "second Adam," reverses the damage done by that sin by redeeming humanity. The theologian and poet John Henry Newman (1801–90) summed this up beautifully in what became the hymn "Praise to the holiest":

O loving wisdom of our God!
When all was sin and shame,
A second Adam to the fight
And to the rescue came.

The writer of "Adam lay ybounden" has turned this idea around, thereby falling into the philosophical trap of presuming that a statement containing a counterfactual can have a truth-value! This means that a statement containing the word "if" cannot be treated for logical purposes as though it were true. I might say, for example, "If it had not rained I would not have got wet," but because the truth of such a statement cannot be verified (it did rain, so how can we know what would have happened if it had not done so?), the statement must be deemed to be false. Thus, while it appears to make sense to say that if it had not rained I would not have got wet, we should not treat this as a logically true statement, because it cannot be verified. It is extremely likely that I would not have got wet, but it cannot be true. It is conceivable that I might have got wet by some other means (someone might have thrown a bucket of water at me).

Such technicalities of language and logic do help us to conclude that the idea that if Adam had not sinned, Jesus would not have come is actually absurd. It is certainly unverifiable and, strictly speaking, is false. Who knows what God would have done? And who are we to decide or guess?

Having demolished the writer's logic, we should at least give credit where it is due: the text is at root a hymn of praise and gratitude to God. The words celebrate the history of salvation and end on a note of thanksgiving. The Bible passage from which the carol draws its inspiration reminds us of the "original" sin of Adam and Eve, whose story shows how easy it is to be tempted by something, especially if it is marketed well. The serpent also uses a certain form of bogus philosophy, based on the idea that if something is forbidden, that must be because it is interesting, and will not do harm but good. Adam and Eve have the maker's instructions to hand, but they prefer the do-it-yourself approach of the snake. Of course, they botch it up, not only for themselves but for all who follow them. And that is why God has to send Christ as redeemer, cleanser, and restorer, for which we continue to give him thanks and praise: "For just as by the one man's disobedience the many were made sinners, so by the one man's obedience the many will be made righteous" (Romans 5:19).

Prayer

Father God, we thank you that you sent your Son Jesus to rescue us from the shame of sin and the fear of death. By your gracious Spirit, teach us the truth of the story of salvation, that we may be released from the bonds of fallen humanity, always free to offer you thanks and praise, this and every day. Amen.

O come, O come, Emmanuel! Part One

Take heed, be quiet, do not fear, and do not let your heart be faint
because of these two smouldering stumps of firebrands, because of the
fierce anger of Rezin and Aram and the son of Remaliah. . . . On that day
the root of Jesse shall stand as a signal to the peoples; the nations shall
inquire of him, and his dwelling shall be glorious. . . . I will place on his
shoulder the key of the house of David; he shall open, and no
one shall shut; he shall shut, and no one shall open. . . .
But for you who revere my name the sun of righteousness shall rise, with
healing in its wings. You shall go out leaping like calves from the stall.
—Isaiah 7:4, 11:10, 22:22; Malachi 4:2

O come, O come, Emmanuel!
Redeem thy captive Israel,
That into exile drear is gone
Far from the face of God's dear Son.
      Rejoice! Rejoice! Emmanuel
      Shall come to thee, O Israel.

O come, thou Wisdom from on high!
Who madest all in earth and sky,
Creating man from dust and clay:
To us reveal salvation's way.

O come, O come, Adonai,
Who in thy glorious majesty
From Sinai's mountain, clothed with awe,
Gavest thy folk the ancient law.

O come, thou Root of Jesse! draw
The quarry from the lion's claw;
From those dread caverns of the grave,
From nether hell, thy people save.

O come, thou Lord of David's Key!
The royal door fling wide and free;
Safeguard for us the heavenward road,
And bar the way to death's abode.

O come, O come, thou Dayspring bright!
Pour on our souls thy healing light;
Dispel the long night's lingering gloom,
And pierce the shadows of the tomb.

O come, Desire of nations! show
Thy kingly reign on earth below;
Thou Cornerstone, uniting all,
Restore the ruin of our fall.

Words: Eighteenth century, trans. T.A. Lacey (1853–1931)
Music: VENI EMMANUEL, adapted from a French Missal by Thomas
Helmore (1811–90)

This season of Advent not only has us looking forward to the return of Christ, but we also look back in order to look forward. The birth of Jesus was itself looked forward to, and as we remind ourselves that he is due to return, we remember some of those prophecies that were to predict his birth in Bethlehem. Not only do they come from the Old Testament, but some of them became enshrined as antiphons (brief texts for liturgical use before and after canticles) even after the New Testament period. The Magnificat is said or sung every day at Evening Prayer, but in the run-up to Christmas, these special verses (the "Advent antiphons"), recalling the prophecies associated with Mary's acceptance of her calling to be the mother of Jesus, were added, giving extra poignancy to the oft-sung text. There is therefore a slight irony in the fact that while "O come, O come, Emmanuel" is a great Advent hymn, it is not ideally suited to the beginning of Advent after all. It is most appropriate as an end-of-Advent hymn, to be sung when one of the verses might coincide with the appropriate antiphon for the particular day.

The antiphons date from the sixth or seventh century, and there were seven of them, according to this scheme:

December 17: O Sapientia

O Wisdom, which camest out of the mouth of the Most High, and reachest from one end to another, mightily and sweetly ordering all things: come and teach us the way of prudence.

December 18: O Adonai

O Adonai, and Leader of the house of Israel, who appearedst in the bush to Moses in a flame of fire, and gavest him the Law in Sinai: come and deliver us with an outstretched arm.

December 19: O Radix Jesse

O Root of Jesse, which standest for an ensign of the people, at whom kings shall shut their mouths, to whom the Gentiles shall seek: come and deliver us, and tarry not.

December 20: O Clavis David

O Key of David and Scepter of the house of Israel; that openest, and no man shutteth, and shuttest, and no man openeth: come and bring the prisoner out of the prisonhouse, and him that sitteth in darkness and the shadow of death.

December 21: O Oriens

O Dayspring, Brightness of Light Everlasting, and Sun of Righteousness: come and enlighten him that sitteth in darkness and the shadow of death.

December 22: O Rex Gentium

O King of the Nations, and their Desire; the Cornerstone, who makest both one: come and save mankind, whom thou formedst of clay.

December 23: O Emmanuel

O Emmanuel, our King and Lawgiver, the Desire of all nations, and their Salvation: come and save us, O Lord our God.

The texts of the antiphons themselves are rich in meaning and resonate with Scripture. Each addresses God by a different name. Wisdom, the first name to be used, draws on a great tradition in the Bible of personifying the figure of Wisdom in feminine terms: "Happy are those who find wisdom, and those who get understanding, for her income is better than silver, and her revenue better than gold" (Proverbs 3:13–14). The desire for the character of Wisdom to teach us is very much in the tradition of the book of Proverbs.

The antiphon O Adonai refers to the Hebrew name for God (Lord), and reminds us of the encounter of Moses with God in the burning bush and of the giving of the tablets of the Ten Commandments. The outstretched arm reminds us of God telling Moses to stretch out his arm each time a plague was to befall the Egyptians, and ultimately of God showing strength with his arm in releasing them. The same idea of God's powerful arm is mentioned by Mary in the Magnificat.

The root of Jesse is mentioned in Isaiah 11 and the key of David in Isaiah 22. The "shadow of death" reminds us of Psalm 23, and the release of the prisoners reminds us of Jesus quoting Isaiah 61 in Luke 4:18. "Dayspring" is a word often associated with dawn, as in Zechariah's prophecy uttered at the birth of John the Baptist, and also with the idea of Christ as the "morning star." Christ as cornerstone is a familiar phrase, found in Ephesians 2:20 and 1 Peter 2:6. The final "O Emmanuel" antiphon is the climactic one, resounding as it does with the prophecy from Isaiah 7:14: "The young woman . . . shall name him Immanuel."

These Latin "Advent antiphons," as they became known, evolved into the hymn "Veni, veni, Emmanuel," of which various translations of "O come, O come, Emmanuel" are the surviving English versions. The first translation was made by Cardinal John Henry Newman in 1836, and John Mason Neale followed suit in 1851. It is actually his own revision of these words that we find in some hymn books, while the words printed here are taken from a different text used in the *New English Hymnal*. Often today we hear the hymn with verses sung in unison, rather as the plainsong would have been, but with rich harmony used for the refrains. This may represent for us something of the complex blend that makes up today's Advent. There is the simple, penitential message of a promised savior, who came and will come again, but there is also the richness and splendor of Christmas, beckoning us from every shop window and carol service as we advance further into December.

Prayer

O come Emmanuel, Key of David, Root of Jesse, Dayspring on high, and reveal yourself as Lord of all the nations. To you we call, Lord Jesus, whose name is above all names, rejoicing in the salvation that you have won for us by your humble birth, sacrificial death, and glorious resurrection. May you reign in glory, in heaven and on earth, now and always. Amen.

"When you see Jerusalem surrounded by armies, then know that its desolation has come near. Then those in Judea must flee to the mountains, and those inside the city must leave it, and those out in the country must not enter it; for these are days of vengeance, as a fulfilment of all that is written. Woe to those who are pregnant and to those who are nursing infants in those days! For there will be great distress on the earth and wrath against this people; they will fall by the edge of the sword and be taken away as captives among all nations; and Jerusalem will be trampled on by the Gentiles, until the times of the Gentiles are fulfilled.

"There will be signs in the sun, the moon, and the stars, and on the earth distress among nations confused by the roaring of the sea and the waves. People will faint from fear and foreboding of what is coming upon the world, for the powers of the heavens will be shaken. Then they will see 'the Son of Man coming in a cloud' with power and great glory. Now when these things begin to take place, stand up and raise your heads, because your redemption is drawing near."
—Luke 21:20–28

"O come, O come, Emmanuel" has inspired a great deal of music. It is the hymn that we most associate with Advent, so much so that we only have to hear a few notes from it to be reminded of the season. I remember the first time I preached in St. Paul's Cathedral after having gone there in 1998 as Succentor. My lot fell to preach at a Sunday eucharist in the middle of August, and the text for the service was a well-known Advent text, Luke 12:32–40 (See "Thou whose almighty Word," p. 29).

As is the usual custom in large cathedrals, the Gospel book is carried down the nave, so that it is read from within the body of the congregation after Alleluias have been sung. This done, the small procession makes its way back to the altar, and the preacher climbs the steps to the pulpit, which is raised about ten feet off the ground. While these very practical liturgical movements are taking place, it is traditional for the organist to improvise, playing music that forms his or her personal response to what has been read.

On this August day in question, John Scott, organist at the time, was playing, and as the procession returned to the altar and I made my hesitant way up the steps for the first time, he played gently, but recognizably, the first few notes of the tune of "O come, O come, Emmanuel." The congregation would have been taken by surprise, undoubtedly, it being summertime, but then the music moved away from the theme and built up, until after about two minutes the theme returned, with other notes flying all around, a trumpet blazing "O come, O come, Emmanuel" through sparkling notes of summer. By this time, I was in the pulpit, admiring the virtuosity, the inventiveness, and the profundity of this musical commentary on what had just been read. As I stood there, looking down the length of St. Paul's, I wondered if there really was any point in saying anything, for in a way it had already all been said with the voice of the organ. While there is no recording of that brief moment of musical theology, it is one of my abiding memories of ministering in that unique and special place. Such can be the power of meaningful music.

God sent his Son Jesus Christ as the harmonic resolution of the discord and cacophony of human sin. Yet the glories of incarnation produced only a partial resolution, interrupted and tainted by crucifixion and redeemed through resurrection. This closure on the eighth day of creation, when Christ rose and made all things new, breaking the chains of death and setting his people free, has yet to be fully realized. There are notes still to be played, chords yet to sound in the great concerto that is the dialogue between God and Creation. In this "middle" time, between Easter salvation and final return, we have plenty of music resounding in our ears, but we need some melodic and harmonic resolutions to make all things good, and to complete the whole.

This is what Advent is about, and it is what impels us to sing, at any time of year, "O come, O come, Emmanuel"!

Prayer
Shake the powers of heaven, O Lord, with drumbeats of glory, and rain down upon us the glittering light of your love, so that the beats of our hearts may reverberate in anticipation of the eternal dialogue you have prepared for us, when heaven and earth shall pass away and all shall enter into the everlasting harmony of your kingdom. Amen.

Once in royal David's city

In those days a decree went out from Emperor Augustus that all the world should be registered. This was the first registration and was taken while Quirinius was governor of Syria. All went to their own towns to be registered. Joseph also went from the town of Nazareth in Galilee to Judea, to the city of David called Bethlehem, because he was descended from the house and family of David. He went to be registered with Mary, to whom he was engaged and who was expecting a child. While they were there, the time came for her to deliver her child. And she gave birth to her firstborn son and wrapped him in bands of cloth, and laid him in a manger, because there was no place for them in the inn.
—Luke 2:1–7

Once in royal David's city
Stood a lowly cattle shed,
Where a mother laid her baby
In a manger for his bed;
Mary was the mother mild,
Jesus Christ her little child.

He came down to earth from heaven
Who is God and Lord of all;
And his shelter was a stable,
And his cradle was a stall;
With the poor and mean and lowly
Lived on earth our Savior holy.

And through all his wondrous childhood
He would honor and obey,
Love and watch the lowly maiden,

In whose gentle arms he lay:
Christian children all must be
Mild, obedient, good as he.

For he is our childhood's pattern,
Day by day like us he grew;
He was little, weak and helpless,
Tears and smiles like us he knew;
And he feeleth for our sadness,
And he shareth in our gladness.

And our eyes at last shall see him,
Through his own redeeming love;
For that child so dear and gentle
Is our Lord in heaven above;
And he leads his children on
To the place where he is gone.

Not in that poor lowly stable,
With the oxen standing by
We shall see him; but in heaven,
Set at God's right hand on high
Where like stars, his children crowned
All in white shall wait around.

Words: C.F. Alexander (1818–95)
Music: IRBY, H.J. Gauntlett (1805–76)

B irth is a miracle, enfleshed millions of times each year in so many places and ways. Clinics with water-birth pools and the latest technologies are de rigueur all over the Western world, and mothers are given lessons in pain management, advised to have "birthing partners," and are generally informed (sometimes too much) about what is going on and what could go wrong. The jargon of "epidural" and "c-section" is so familiar to expectant mothers these days and, as with many things, the intention is to facilitate choice and control. Pregnancy and childbirth are far safer than they used to be, but there is still a fair bit of trepidation about!

In some less technologically equipped parts of the world, giving birth is little different from the way it would have been in first-century Palestine. There is no maternity leave or benefit (no "job" to have leave from!), and only certain cultures promote rest for the expectant mother. Back in first-century Palestine, poor Mary had to trek from Nazareth to Bethlehem, a journey of about 70 miles. After bouncing along on a beast of burden for up to ten days, it is little surprise that her labor began and she was soon delivered of her Savior son. It makes one wonder whether Jesus was born prematurely.

It was not so different in the middle of the nineteenth century, when Frances Alexander was writing "Once in royal David's city." Victorian England had a high rate of infant mortality: in Sheffield, for example, the General Infirmary recorded 11,944 deaths between 1837 and 1842, half of which were of children under the age of five. Statistics such as these help us to understand part of the spiritual agenda of this carol. With so many children dying young, the verses at the end of the carol can be seen in a different light. To us today, the idea that Jesus "leads his children" to heaven, where "all in white" they wait around, crowned as angels, is a rather strange, sentimental, even unsatisfactory picture of heaven. But to those many who had lost little ones, these words provided some comfort, convincing them that those brief lives were not in vain.

Some people today feel that the words are too outdated for modern use. The idea that "Christian children all must be mild, obedient, good as he" rankles with some worshipers, as such sentiments are redolent of the Victorian Sunday school with its dry biblical teaching through catechism and discipline (although one might ask why children should not be obedient). Mrs. Alexander was trying to help, not only by writing singable hymns but also by conveying essential Christian truths through her words. "Once in royal David's city" was specifically intended to teach that major part of the creed: "I believe in Jesus Christ, his only Son our Lord, who was conceived by the Holy Spirit, born of the Virgin Mary." In writing this carol, she demonstrated both her love of children and her understanding of the humanity of Christ. Like many youth workers today, her heart was very much in the mission and evangelization of young people, always striving to bring the gospel up to date for each and every generation.

Her words, whether we consider them old-fashioned or not, are rich in scriptural overtones. While the first verse sets out in straightforward terms the circumstances of Christ's birth, the second stanza introduces a reference to the kenotic (self-emptying) Christ that we encounter in Philippians 2:5–8. The stanza goes on to remind us of Christ's earthly poverty, as referred to in 2 Corinthians 8:9: "though he was rich, yet for your sakes he became poor, so that by his poverty you might become rich." The next verse reminds us of Jesus' sinlessness, as set out in 1 John 3:5: "You know that he was revealed to take away sins, and in him there is no sin." Though sinless, he was also human: thus, like us, he knew of the joys and pains (tears and smiles) of human existence, and this is touched upon in the fourth verse.

The fifth verse reminds us of the end of the story, of Christ risen, ascended, glorified. Christ reigning in heaven is not a childish fantasy but a scriptural truth. "All in white, who wait around" is perhaps an unfortunate description of those who have had their robes washed in the blood of the lamb (Revelation 4:4; 7:14), but it is clearly Mrs. Alexander's pastoral vision that the souls of deceased children go to be with God, casting their star-like crowns before him as they enjoy the eternal bliss of heaven. It may be a mawkish vision with which to conclude a delightful and enduring hymn, but it is perhaps churlish to omit this verse, as it points us, firmly rooted in the earthbound stable, upwards to that higher, purer place where there shall be no more tears—a new heaven and earth, presided over by our Lord Jesus Christ.

Prayer

Father God, whose Son Jesus Christ came down to earth from heaven, hear our prayers for all who are weak and helpless. By the power of your redeeming love, lead us your children to share in the gladness of that day when all tears shall be turned to smiles in your heavenly city, where, with saints and angels attending, you reign in glory for ever. Amen.

December 20 **Gabriel's message**

In the sixth month the angel Gabriel was sent by God to a town in Galilee called Nazareth, to a virgin engaged to a man whose name was Joseph, of the house of David. The virgin's name was Mary. And he came to her and said, "Greetings, favored one! The Lord is with you." But she was much perplexed by his words and pondered what sort of greeting this might be. The angel said to her, "Do not be afraid, Mary, for you have found favor with God. And now, you will conceive in your womb and bear a son, and you will name him Jesus. He will be great, and will be called the Son of the Most High, and the Lord God will give to him the throne of his ancestor David. He will reign over the house of Jacob for ever, and of his kingdom there will be no end." Mary said to the angel, "How can this be, since I am a virgin?" The angel said to her, "The Holy Spirit will come upon you, and the power of the Most High will overshadow you; therefore the child to be born will be holy; he will be called Son of God. And now, your relative Elizabeth in her old age has also conceived a son; and this is the sixth month for her who was said to be barren. For nothing will be impossible with God." Then Mary said, "Here am I, the servant of the Lord; let it be with me according to your word." Then the angel departed from her.

—Luke 1:26–38

The angel Gabriel from heaven came,
his wings as drifted snow, his eyes as flame
"All hail," said he, "thou lowly maiden Mary,
most highly favored lady!" Gloria!

"For lo! a blessed Mother thou shalt be,
all generations laud and honor thee.
Thy Son shall be Emmanuel, by seers foretold,
most highly favored lady!" Gloria!

Then gentle Mary meekly bowed her head;
"To me be as it pleaseth God," she said;
"My soul shall laud and magnify his holy name."
Most highly favored lady! Gloria!

Of her, Emmanuel, the Christ, was born
in Bethlehem, all on a Christmas morn.
And Christian folk throughout the world will ever say,
"Most highly favored lady!" Gloria!

Words: Sabine Baring Gould (1834–1924)
Music: Basque traditional

Waiting for a baby to be born is a strange experience, though in different ways for mother and father. For both parents there is a kind of unreality: it seems it can't be really happening, even though, as every day goes by, the physical evidence becomes more real. It is strange enough for us today, knowing how babies develop in the womb, and able to take advantage of hospitals, midwives, and scanning machines, all of which can confirm or dispel hopes or fears, but what must it have been like for Mary and Joseph? For Mary, like any human mother, the idea and manifestation of pregnancy is natural, but utterly strange. Her body would be taken over by another being, growing, moving, becoming, inside her. As time went by, the spiritual words of an angel would be confirmed by the physical kicking of a human baby. Church tradition dates the Feast of the Annunciation to March 25, a very precise nine months before December 25! And in Luke's Gospel we read that the angel tells Mary that her cousin Elizabeth is now in her "sixth month." If this is all correct, then

Jesus would have been born nine months later, and John the Baptist would then have been six months old.

Mary's response to the angel, which has been handed on to us as the Magnificat ("My soul magnifies the Lord. . . ."), is an inspiring profession of faith and acceptance. Mary's "yes" to God has helped generations to be strong, committed, and resolute in the face of poverty, war, persecution, and doubt. As her body accepts the inevitable restrictions and discomforts that childbearing will involve, her spirit also affirms the route on which she and the whole of humanity are about to embark. The journey she makes through pregnancy involves her children's children, spiritually speaking. In bearing the child of God, she reminds us that we are the children of God, spiritually descended from the same heavenly Father.

There are quotations from the Magnificat to be found in this carol, in the third verse. In a brief, two-minute piece of music, we have the heart of the Annunciation story. We hear of Gabriel arriving and telling Mary the good news, and there is a lovely foretaste of the later visitation to the shepherds as the refrain Gloria is used at the end of each verse. The annunciation is the first step toward that day when the angels will sing "glory," and all humanity join in, as the promised Messiah, the Emmanuel, the Savior, is born. While the carol is rooted in the scriptural text, there is an opening out in the last verse, where the focus moves away from describing the event of the Annunciation to the angel telling Mary that one day "Christian folk throughout the world will ever say, 'Most highly favored lady!'" This brings the story into the present, just as we have been taken to the past in remembering that very strange and disconcerting message that Gabriel brought her, all those years ago.

The words come from a traditional Basque carol, and were translated by the Reverend Sabine Baring Gould, author of the hymn "Onward, Christian soldiers." The charming tune of "Gabriel's message" also originates in the Basque region. As with the story of salvation itself, there is both control and a certain inevitability and pace to the proceedings. This is heady stuff, we might feel, enough to make anyone jumpy, but all is kept on the rails by a sure, steady foundation of faith, on which Mary herself is drawn along. Her example gives us the confidence to believe and the desire to follow.

Prayer

Heavenly Father, as you sent an angel to Mary bearing good news for all people, enlighten and enrich us with the good news of your love for us all; and as we are reminded of the birth of your Son Jesus Christ, come and dwell in our hearts, that we too may leap to your voice and live our lives in the steady rhythm of mercy on which our faith is founded. Amen.

Ave Maria

In those days Mary set out and went with haste to a Judean town in the hill country, where she entered the house of Zechariah and greeted Elizabeth. When Elizabeth heard Mary's greeting, the child leapt in her womb. And Elizabeth was filled with the Holy Spirit and exclaimed with a loud cry, "Blessed are you among women, and blessed is the fruit of your womb. And why has this happened to me, that the mother of my Lord comes to me? For as soon as I heard the sound of your greeting, the child in my womb leapt for joy. And blessed is she who believed that there would be a fulfilment of what was spoken to her by the Lord."
—Luke 1:39–45

Hail Mary, full of grace, the Lord is with thee. Blessed art thou amongst women and blessed is the fruit of thy womb Jesus. (Holy Mary, Mother of God, pray for us sinners, now and at the hour of our death. Amen.)

This text must be one of the most common in Western music, not only because of its central place in Roman Catholic devotion but also because of its pastoral, maternal, and thoroughly human focus. Whatever we may think of the theological controversies that surround its meaning and direction, there is no doubt that the Ave Maria has inspired and comforted countless generations of Christians.

In order to make up our own minds about what we think of it, we need to divide it into three parts. First, the opening words come from Luke 1:28: "Greetings, favored one! The Lord is with you." These are the words with which the angel Gabriel greets Mary at the Annunciation. The second part quotes Elizabeth's words: "Blessed are you among women, and blessed is the fruit of your womb" (v. 42). To this has been added the name of Jesus. The third section is the most controversial, as it has little if any scriptural origin. The Roman Catholic Council of Trent determined in the sixteenth century that the phrase "Holy Mary, Mother of God, pray for us now and at the hour of our death" was composed by the church, while the term "Mother of God" originated in the Council of Ephesus in AD 431 and was used in the Creed of Chalcedon. The purpose then was not so much to elevate the status of Mary as "God bearer" (Theotokos), but to emphasize the truly dual nature of Christ as divine and human.

Many people feel uneasy with the Hail Mary, as praying "to" the Virgin Mary is implied in the prayer. Christ is our intercessor, and it is he through whom our prayers are offered: "Consequently he is able for all time to save those who approach God through him, since he always lives to make intercession for them" (Hebrews 7:25). In Protestant theology, there is simply no need to offer prayers either to or through the Virgin Mary, and so, while some people find no need for the Hail Mary in their devotions, others are offended by it.

The theological hang-up that Jesus' mother sometimes inspires can so easily lead us away from some very simple truths about the young girl from Nazareth whom God called to be the mother of his Son, Jesus Christ our Savior. She accepts God's call and we have every reason to believe that Mary is someone who has received a very special blessing from God.

It comes as no surprise that the Ave Maria has inspired some beautiful music. Many composers have used it, and the versions by Schubert and Gounod are probably the best known today. Choral versions exist too, such as the sublime setting by the sixteenth-century composer Robert Parsons, which opens with a haunting tenor solo and concludes with an extended Amen. Written for six-part choir, it employs only the first two (biblical) parts of the text, thereby avoiding any controversy over the origins of the third section. The brief but equally beautiful setting attributed to the sixteenth-century Spanish composer Tomás Luis de Victoria includes the full text. Other settings of the Ave Maria include that of Anton Bruckner (1824–96), a devout Austrian Catholic, whose unaccompanied choral setting includes the full text, but has an early climax on the name of Jesus, reminding us that however respectful of Mary we might want to be, Jesus Christ is the focus of our faith.

Music is a great leveler and a means by which opposing views can be reconciled, and to a certain extent the famous and gorgeous setting by Charles Gounod (1818–93) embodies this truth. Often the work is described as being by Bach/Gounod, because the piece that Gounod composed in 1853 was exactly that—a melodic meditation written "above" the first of Bach's Twenty-Four Preludes and Fugues for keyboard (known as *The Well-tempered Clavier*), which the great German composer wrote in 1722. The first of these preludes consists of a simple but inspired set of chord progressions, fanned out as arpeggios, giving a fluid effect, as if bearing us on a journey. Gounod, inspired by this simple beauty, added the prayer to Mary, fitting the Latin text to sustained notes that float and linger in the ethereal spaces created above Bach's watery harmonic structure.

Bach, who was a committed German Lutheran, composed the *St. Matthew Passion* and cantatas for every Sunday of the church year. Gounod was a devout French Roman Catholic and an expert on the works of Palestrina, and he considered entering the priesthood before settling on a career as organist and composer. His Ave Maria must therefore be seen as one of the greatest ecumenical works known to us—an unplanned collaboration between Lutheranism and Catholicism that gave birth to a moving song that continues to inspire and uplift so many, so often. Dare we suppose that Mary herself would have been pleased that, in spite of all the controversy, a setting of the Ave Maria has quietly crossed ecclesiological boundaries and given pleasure and inspiration to those in sickness and in health, in sorrow and in joy? I think we might!

Prayer

Creator God, we thank you for the example of faith, commitment, and love that you offer to us in the life and witness of Mary. May we, like her, respond to your call and live our lives in your service, seeking always to live in harmony with others, in churches, communities, and nations, for the sake of her Son, Jesus Christ our Lord. Amen.

Masters in this hall

And Mary said,

"My soul magnifies the Lord,

and my spirit rejoices in God my Savior,

for he has looked with favor on the lowliness of his servant.

Surely, from now on all generations will call me blessed;

for the Mighty One has done great things for me,

and holy is his name.

His mercy is for those who fear him

from generation to generation.

He has shown strength with his arm;

he has scattered the proud in the thoughts of their hearts.

He has brought down the powerful from their thrones,

and lifted up the lowly;

he has filled the hungry with good things,

and sent the rich away empty.

He has helped his servant Israel,

in remembrance of his mercy,

according to the promise he made to our ancestors,

to Abraham and to his descendants for ever."

—Luke 1:46–55

Masters in this hall

Hear ye news today,

Brought from over seas

And ever you I pray.

> Noel, Noel, Noel
>
> Noel sing we clear!
>
> Holpen all the folk on earth
>
> Born the Son of God so dear!
>
> Noel, Noel,

Noel sing we loud
God to day hath poor folk raised
and cast a-down the proud.

Going o'er the hills,
Through the milk-white snow,
Heard I ewes bleat
While the wind did blow.
Noel, Noel, Noel...

Shepherds many an one
Sat among the sheep,
No man spake more word
Than they had been asleep.
Noel, Noel, Noel...

Quoth I, "Fellows mine,
Why this guise sit ye?
Making but dull cheer,
Shepherds though ye be?"
Noel, Noel, Noel...

Shepherds should of right
Leap and dance and sing,
Thus to see ye sit,
Is a right strange thing."
Noel, Noel, Noel...

Quoth these fellows then,
"To Bethlem town we go,
To see a mighty lord
Lie in manger low."
Noel, Noel, Noel...

"How name ye this lord,
Shepherds?" then said I.
"Very God," they said,
"Come from Heaven high."
Noel, Noel, Noel...

This is Christ the Lord,
Masters be ye glad!
Christmas is come in,
And no folk should be sad.
Noel, Noel, Noel...

Words: William Morris (1834–96)
Music: French traditional

The words of this rather quaint-sounding carol are not as old as they appear. The man who wrote them is famous for his artistic designs, his wallpaper, his political views, and his prose and poetry, but his small contribution to the Christmas carol repertoire has been largely overlooked. For the author of this carol is in fact William Morris, the famous social critic, artist, and writer of Victorian England.

Morris' carol "Masters in this hall" represents a tiny part of his artistic output. It was first published in 1860 in *Nine Ancient and Goodly Carols for the Merry Tide of Christmas*. The tune was suggested by the architect Edmund Sedding (1836–68), who published the volume. Algernon Charles Swinburne (1837–1909), himself the author of the obscure carol "Thou whose birth on earth," described Morris' carol as "one of the co-equal three finest . . . in the language," and so it was also included in A. H. Bullen's *A Christmas Garland; Carols and Poems from the Fifteenth Century to the Present* in 1885.

Morris' predilection for all things medieval can clearly be detected in the carol. The language, so admired by Swinburne, is archaic, but it tells that timeless tale of the shepherds traveling to Bethlehem to greet the Christ-child. The text describes a dialogue between narrator and shepherds, interposing a chorus in which we can detect a hint of Morris' socialist leanings: "Noel sing we loud, God to day hath poor folk raised and cast a-down the proud." Such sentiments might well appeal to one who believed that we are equal inasmuch as we all need food, clothes, and shelter, and that it must follow that if anyone is not able to satisfy their needs in these respects there is something wrong with society. The gospel, to Morris, was good news to the poor, and this carol emphasizes that aspect in each and every refrain.

The link with Mary's words at the Annunciation (the Magnificat) is clear. Mary's song promises a new world order, a new freedom, a new dawn of salvation, peace and joy. She anticipates the "Gloria" of the shepherds, and Morris' account of meeting the shepherds reminds us of it. For Morris, the "Masters in this hall" might have been the bourgeois wealthy who need to pay attention to the gospel for the poor and lowly (such as shepherds), in order to promote equality of wealth and resources for all people. Socialism and Christianity are by no means opposed in outlook, and it could be said that the "official" manifestations of both have had their ups and downs over the years. Worldviews are so often damaged by those who adhere to them.

When we consider Mary and her response to the angel's greeting, we have an even greater example to admire. Her words are humble and comforting, but also challenging to all who follow her in the path of faith. Mary's "yes" to God is a submissive "yes," but at the same time she takes control and responsibility for the very act of service to which it leads. In her response to Gabriel, Mary identifies and accepts the will of God. She could have said "no," which means that in choosing to accept, she not only preserves her human freedom but also turns her acquiescence into an almost defiant "yes" that affirms the poverty and weakness of many, for whom the coming of the Messiah will be a release from captivity. Mary knows this, and she accepts it with joy, gratitude, and a certain defiance that has made her words a touchstone for the poor and downtrodden ever since.

Prayer

Mighty God and Father of us all, we rejoice in your salvation by which you bless the world. You look favorably on all who are impoverished in mind, body, or spirit, and in your holiness you do great things for your people. Have mercy on all who fear the strength of your arm, and scatter the foolishness of pride, prejudice, and power. Fill us instead with good things, according to the promises you have revealed in Jesus Christ, your Son, our Lord. Amen.

Now the birth of Jesus the Messiah took place in this way. When his mother Mary had been engaged to Joseph, but before they lived together, she was found to be with child from the Holy Spirit. Her husband Joseph, being a righteous man and unwilling to expose her to public disgrace, planned to dismiss her quietly. But just when he had resolved to do this, an angel of the Lord appeared to him in a dream and said, "Joseph, son of David, do not be afraid to take Mary as your wife, for the child conceived in her is from the Holy Spirit. She will bear a son, and you are to name him Jesus, for he will save his people from their sins." All this took place to fulfil what had been spoken by the Lord through the prophet: "Look, the virgin shall conceive and bear a son, and they shall name him Emmanuel," which means, "God is with us." When Joseph awoke from sleep, he did as the angel of the Lord commanded him; he took her as his wife, but had no marital relations with her until she had borne a son; and he named him Jesus.

—Matthew 1:18–25

PART ONE

Joseph was an old man,
And an old man was he,
When he married Mary
In the land of Galilee.

And as they were walking
Through an orchard so good,
Where were cherries and berries
As red as any blood.

O then bespoke Mary,
With words both meek and mild,

"Pluck me one cherry, Joseph,
For that I am with child."

Go to the tree then Mary,
And it shall bow to thee
And you shall gather cherries
By one, by two, by three.

Then bow'd down the highest tree
Unto our Lady's hand:
"See," Mary cried, "See, Joseph,
I have cherries at command!"

"O eat your cherries, Mary,
O eat your cherries now;
O eat your cherries, Mary,
That grow upon the bough."

Then Mary pluck'd a cherry
As red as any blood;
Mary went she homewards
All with her heavy load.

Words and music: English traditional

We know little about Joseph, and it is often assumed that he had died by the time Jesus reached maturity. This is why, in the Roman Catholic Church, he is revered as the patron saint of a "good death." He is also venerated as the patron of the family and, more recently, as Joseph "the worker": the carpenter, who labored at the plane and the lathe, educating his son Jesus in that trade (see Matthew 13:55).

We do know that Joseph was a decent man whose engagement to Mary had been properly made. This meant that although she was still living with her parents, they were legally bound, such that if he had died in that period, she would have become a widow. Sex was not permitted before marriage, so she should not have been pregnant. Given that she was, Joseph would have known that she could be stoned, but also that the custom at that time would be to divorce her. He could do this publicly, by demanding a trial, and since he was a righteous or law-abiding citizen, his contemporaries might have expected him to do so. It is therefore not his righteousness that makes him protect her: a "righteous" man would have put her on trial.

Joseph not only knows his law, being a righteous man, but he also knows his Scripture. When the angel quotes from Isaiah 7:14, it is a reminder to him. It is as though the angel is saying, "Joseph, don't worry. You remember the old prophecy about a virgin conceiving and a Messiah being born? Well, this is it!" Joseph does not do as he is told merely because an angel tells him to, but because he knows the score: it is revealed to him how he fits in and what is going on in the divine plan. It is, then, no surprise that he does as he is commanded and marries Mary.

Given what his contemporaries expected him to do, Joseph is courageous. He is risking a scandal, not so much because others might suspect that he is not Jesus' father, but because they would assume that he is, and that intercourse had taken place before marriage. This is why Matthew specifically tells us that no such thing happened. Matthew not only emphasizes the miraculous nature of Jesus' conception, he also protects Joseph's honor in the event of future doubt. For then, as now, people are prone to gossip, to draw conclusions from half-facts and casual acquaintance.

Thus reputations are ruined and falsehoods spread. Fortunately, Matthew is clear and precise as he reveals the truth of Jesus' birth.

The medieval carol that tells the story of Joseph's dilemma appears in various versions and of different lengths. It is helpful to think of it as being in three parts: the first concerns a slightly mythical account of how Mary and Joseph related to one another when she told him she was pregnant; the second part deals with the events of Christmas Eve; and the third part is more Lenten in feel.

There are far too many verses recounting a conversation between Mary and Joseph to reproduce them all here. One verse that is rarely sung touches a harsh note as Joseph criticizes Mary for having got pregnant:

O then bespoke Joseph
With words so unkind,
"Let him pluck thee a cherry
That brought thee with child."

Joseph repents of his barbed words when the minor miracle of the tree bowing to her occurs. On one level it all seems a bit trivial, but there is a sort of underlying humanity that we can respect, as we are here being given a fictitious glimpse into their relationship. It must be tough being told that your spouse is carrying someone else's child, and Joseph would have undoubtedly gone through some emotional turmoil.

In Joseph, we see a tendency to be merciful in the face of the law—an ability to respond to situations with compassion, consideration, and carefulness. It is something that Jesus himself was later to advocate, and it is an approach that is characteristic of Christianity. In a world full of laws and regulations, we should remember Joseph, who knew how to be flexible for the sake of another's good.

Prayer

Heavenly Father, as you sent an angel to Joseph, that his will and yours might be united, fill us with the same courage, compassion, and mercy that we find in Joseph, and just as he adopted Jesus as his own, so may we be adopted as your sons and daughters, in the faith and love of Jesus Christ, your Son, our Lord. Amen.

Hark! the herald angels sing

In that region there were shepherds living in the fields, keeping watch over their flock by night. Then an angel of the Lord stood before them, and the glory of the Lord shone around them, and they were terrified. But the angel said to them, "Do not be afraid; for see—I am bringing you good news of great joy for all the people: to you is born this day in the city of David a Savior, who is the Messiah, the Lord. This will be a sign for you: you will find a child wrapped in bands of cloth and lying in a manger." And suddenly there was with the angel a multitude of the heavenly host, praising God and saying, "Glory to God in the highest heaven, and on earth peace among those whom he favors!"
—Luke 2:8–14

Hark! the herald angels sing
Glory to the newborn King;
Peace on earth and mercy mild,
God and sinners reconciled:
Joyful all ye nations rise,
Join the triumph of the skies,
With the angelic host proclaim,
Christ is born in Bethlehem:
Hark! the herald angels sing
Glory to the new-born King.

Christ, by highest heaven adored,
Christ, the everlasting Lord,
Late in time behold him come,
Offspring of a Virgin's womb!
Veiled in flesh the Godhead see,
Hail the incarnate Deity!

Pleased as man with man to dwell,
Jesus, our Emmanuel:
Hark! the herald angels sing
Glory to the new-born King.

Hail the heaven-born Prince of Peace!
Hail the Sun of Righteousness!
Light and life to all he brings,
Risen with healing in his wings;
Mild, he lays his glory by,
Born that man no more may die,
Born to raise the sons of earth,
Born to give them second birth:
Hark! the herald angels sing
Glory to the new-born King.

Words: Charles Wesley (1707–88), George Whitfield (1714–70),
Martin Madan (1726–90) and William Hayman Cummings (1831–1915)
Music: MENDELSSOHN, from a chorus by Felix Mendelssohn-Bartholdy
(1809–47), adapted by William Hayman Cummings

The carol we now know as "Hark! the herald angels sing" did not start life as such, and required at least four people to bring it to its current form. Wesley's original, written as a Christmas Day hymn and first published in 1739, is made up of ten four-line verses, rather than the longer eight-line verses with refrain which we have now.

It is interesting to note that in the original version of Wesley's, the heavens ring with the phrase "Glory to the King of kings," echoing Luke's "Glory to God in the highest heaven." George Whitfield, who had been a student with Wesley, changed this to

"Glory to the new-born King" in 1753. His fairly revolutionary Calvinist position was not compatible with Wesley's gentler reforming approach, which eventually bore fruit in the Methodist movement that he and his brother John inspired. Whitfield maintained the four-line verses of Wesley's original, but changed the angels' emphasis: "Glory to the new-born King" means something slightly but significantly different from "Glory to the King of kings." In the Gospel account the angels praise God, whereas in "Hark! the herald angels sing," they are inaccurately described as praising Jesus. Furthermore, Luke does not say that the angels "sing," and so it may well be that this reinterpretation by Whitfield has emphasized the popular but unscriptural picture of angels singing the Gloria. ("While shepherds watched" also implies that they sang.)

Whitfield also cut the final verses, which are now largely forgotten:

Come, desire of nations, come,
Fix in us thy humble home;
Rise, the woman's conquering seed,
Bruise in us the serpent's head.

Now display thy saving power,
Ruin'd nature now restore;
Now in mystic union join
Thine to ours, and ours to thine.

Adam's likeness, Lord, efface,
Stamp thy image in its place.
Second Adam from above,
Reinstate us in thy love.

Let us thee, though lost, regain,
Thee, the life, the inner man:
O, to all thyself impart,
Form'd in each believing heart.

There is some real theological insight in these neglected verses. First of all we notice the Advent antiphon "Come, desire of nations, come," followed by a reference to the fall, with the serpent bruising the heel of humanity and Adam bruising its head (Genesis 3:15). Wesley cleverly alters the meaning, asking that the serpent in us (sin) should be bruised (defeated) by Christ, the second Adam, who reinstates us as beloved sons and daughters of God. In the restoration of sinful humanity to a state of grace through the incarnation of Christ, the joining of divine and human nature is also achieved. Consequently, that which was lost (salvation) is gained and a new life is granted to all believers.

The tune we now call MENDELSSOHN comes from the second chorus, "Gott ist Licht" ("God is Light"). While there can be no doubt that the marriage of Mendelssohn's tune and the adapted words has been most fortuitous, it is rather ironic that Mendelssohn, while recognizing the value of his tune, felt that it would be unsuitable for sacred words. Similarly, Wesley, when writing the original text, suggested that a slow, solemn tune would fit them best. He refused to sing Whitfield's reworking of his words, furious that he had presumed to alter them to suit his own ends. Nowadays, there would probably be an outcry if someone were to suggest even slight changes, and some attempts to "inclusivize" the language have been coolly received.

"Hark! the herald angels sing" has become part of the institution of Christmas, and while it contains inaccuracies, it also sounds out some wonderful theology, musically reminding us that Jesus, the "new-born King," is "Prince of Peace," "Sun of Righteousness," "Everlasting Lord," "Incarnate Deity," and, best of all, "Emmanuel"—"God with us." Whatever its creators would have thought about the hymn as it currently stands, it endures as a reminder of the great gift that our Father God has given us in his Son Jesus Christ, and which we will celebrate in only a few hours' time.

Prayer

Glory to you, O Christ, our newborn King! By the light and life which you bring, reconciling sinners, be pleased to fix in us your humble home, so that we too may join the triumph of the skies, where in highest heaven you are adored by saints and angels singing your praises, this holy night and always. Amen.

While shepherds watched their flocks by night

When the angels had left them and gone into heaven, the shepherds said to one another, "Let us go now to Bethlehem and see this thing that has taken place, which the Lord has made known to us." So they went with haste and found Mary and Joseph, and the child lying in the manger. When they saw this, they made known what had been told them about this child; and all who heard it were amazed at what the shepherds told them. But Mary treasured all these words and pondered them in her heart. The shepherds returned, glorifying and praising God for all they had heard and seen, as it had been told them.
—Luke 2:15–20

While shepherds watched their flocks by night,
All seated on the ground,
The angel of the Lord came down,
And glory shone around.

"Fear not," said he (for mighty dread
Had seized their troubled mind),
"Glad tidings of great joy I bring
To you and all mankind.

"To you in David's town this day
Is born of David's line
A Savior who is Christ the Lord;
And this shall be the sign:

The heavenly Babe you there shall find
To human view displayed,
All meanly wrapped in swathing bands
And in a manger laid."

Thus spake the Seraph, and forthwith
Appeared a shining throng
Of angels, praising God, who thus
Addressed their joyful song:

"All glory be to God on high,
And to the earth be peace:
Goodwill henceforth from heaven to men
Begin and never cease."

Words: Nahum Tate (1652–1715)
Music: WINCHESTER OLD, Thomas Este's Psalter, 1592; CHRISTMAS,
Georg Frideric Handel (1685–1759)

Merry Christmas! As is right and proper today, we continue the reading about the shepherds abiding in the fields, watching their flocks by night, who are suddenly greeted by the angels in the skies, offering the first ever rendition of the Gloria in Excelsis Deo: "Glory to God in the highest!" This carol is basically a retelling of the Christmas Day Gospel reading. The words date from around 1700, and are by Nahum Tate, an Irishman who settled in London in 1672, becoming Poet Laureate. He was a friend of the poet John Dryden, and met a rather sorry end in a debtor's prison, having become an alcoholic, but he was nevertheless buried in the recently completed St. Paul's Cathedral in London.

Tate is reckoned to have written "While shepherds watched" as part of his contribution to a collaborative work with the Reverend Nicholas Brady entitled *New Version of the Psalms of David, Fitted to the Tunes used in Churches*, which was published in 1696.

The very story that the carol tells is quite strange. Shepherds minding their own business, guarding flocks at night, are bombarded with angelic song from on high, apparently telling them good news that a little baby who has been born in a stable is going to bring about peace and reconciliation. It is not surprising that they were amazed, nor that many since then, and today, find the story so fantastical as to be unbelievable. Yet the story persists, and continues not only to appeal but to strike notes of beauty and chords of truth even into the hearts of cynical twenty-first-century humanity. The pastoral setting of the story, and the spiritual context of salvation in Christ, are closed books to so many today, yet there is something in the angels' song that we still long for and hope for.

As with the carol, there have been so many interpretations, so many different ways of singing the song of salvation, some of which have been better or more beautiful than others, but through it all the truth persists. "While shepherds watched their flocks by night" has had so many different incarnations, and has presented so many possibilities, that it can be hard to remember that ultimately it is a song of good news: good news of salvation brought about in the one and only incarnation of Jesus Christ, the Son of God, who took our flesh so that when we "catch our death," we will not simply be handed back to earth to be eaten by worms and recycled, but will ourselves become caught up in that angelic hymn of praise, offered for the glory of God on earth and in heaven.

Prayer

Glory to you, heavenly Father, for in Christ you have cast away our fear and, by your angels, have brought to us a hope of good-will among all nations. Keep watch over us, the sheep of your pasture, and lead us into all peace until that day when, with angels and archangels, we will sing your praises in the highest heaven, where you reign, with the Spirit and the Son, Jesus Christ our Lord. Amen.

December 26 **Good King Wenceslas**

"Then the king will say to those at his right hand, 'Come, you that are
blessed by my Father, inherit the kingdom prepared for you from the
foundation of the world; for I was hungry and you gave me food, I
was thirsty and you gave me something to drink, I was a stranger and
you welcomed me, I was naked and you gave me clothing, I was sick
and you took care of me, I was in prison and you visited me.' Then
the righteous will answer him, 'Lord, when was it that we saw you
hungry and gave you food, or thirsty and gave you something to
drink? And when was it that we saw you a stranger and welcomed
you, or naked and gave you clothing? And when was it that we saw
you sick or in prison and visited you?' And the king will answer them,
'Truly I tell you, just as you did it to one of the least of these who are
members of my family, you did it to me.'"
—Matthew 25:34–40

Good King Wenceslas looked out
On the Feast of Stephen,
When the snow lay round about,
Deep, and crisp, and even:
Brightly shone the moon that night,
Though the frost was cruel,
When a poor man came in sight,
Gathering winter fuel.

"Hither, page, and stand by me,
If thou knowest it, telling.
Yonder peasant, who is he?
Where and what his dwelling?"
"Sire, he lives a good league hence,
Underneath the mountain,

Right against the forest fence,
By Saint Agnes' fountain."

"Bring me flesh, and bring me wine,
Bring me pine-logs hither:
Thou and I will see him dine,
When we bear them thither."
Page and monarch, forth they went,
Forth they went together;
Through the rude wind's wild lament
And the bitter weather.

"Sire, the night is darker now,
And the wind blows stronger;
Fails my heart, I know not how;
I can go no longer."
"Mark my footsteps, good my page;
Tread thou in them boldly:
Thou shalt find the winter's rage
Freeze thy blood less coldly."

In his master's steps he trod,
Where the snow lay dinted;
Heat was in the very sod
Which the Saint had printed.
Therefore, Christian men, be sure,
Wealth or rank possessing,
Ye who now will bless the poor,
Shall yourselves find blessing.

Words: John Mason Neale (1818–66)
Music: from Piae Cantiones, Theoderici Petri Nylandensis, 1582

This popular carol was written by the prolific English hymn writer John Mason Neale in 1853. Neale translated many Latin hymns, but this one he wrote specifically as a carol to promote a spirit of generosity. Neale felt that the Christian virtue of generosity should be promoted, especially at Christmas time, and he was well aware of the power of hymns and carols to influence people's thinking and behavior. Thus he turned to the old legend of King Wenceslas for a story on which to pin his moral purpose. Before actually writing the words, he chose an appropriate tune from a sixteenth-century tune book from the Finnish cathedral city of Turku, known as *Piae Cantiones*. The tune he chose was originally allied with a Latin text "Tempus adest floridium" ("Spring has unwrapped her flowers"), and some people, among them Ralph Vaughan Williams, have criticized Neale's substitution of what they considered to be "doggerel" for a perfectly good set of springtime words.

Doggerel or not, the text and the popular tune have survived. In the song, we learn only a little about that good king who went out in bitter weather to help the poor, and encouraged his servant who went with him. In reality, Wenceslas was a prince of Bohemia, in what is now the Czech Republic. His story really begins when his grandmother Ludmilla became a Christian. Wenceslas' pagan mother Drahomira ruled Bohemia at the time; the powerful non-Christians resented Ludmilla's influence, and she was murdered in 921. Wenceslas was then still a prince, but he assumed power in 922 when Drahomira was ousted, and he ruled Bohemia as a Christian. He gained a reputation for being friendly to the German realms that neighbored his own, and promoted good order among his citizens. Popular with the people as this approach may have been, it was not liked by his younger brother, Boleslav. In 929, Boleslav invited Wenceslas to stay with him, and, after a quarrel broke out between them, Boleslav's men killed Wenceslas. Consequently, he and his grandmother Ludmilla are revered as martyrs especially in the region around the Czech Republic, for which he became patron saint. The main square in Prague is still named after him.

While historical evidence is a bit thin, Neale would have us believe that Wenceslas was a good, honest, and strongly principled man. The song describes him braving a fierce storm in order to help to feed a hungry neighbor. This practical faith reminds us of the parable of the sheep and the goats, where Jesus very clearly teaches us to look after those in need, to visit the sick and clothe the naked. In Wenceslas' time, there were no doubt many poor, but it is hardly different today. To some extent, the help that the poor and the homeless receive is now better organized, but it is never enough, and organizations such as The Salvation Army and Red Cross at Christmas always seem to need more money and volunteers. Wenceslas' example, immortalized in this carol, is certainly one to follow. People still die of cold in their homes and on the streets of our towns and cities in twenty-first-century America, and so we should be generous with our money, our time, and our prayers, as we are able.

Although Neale specifically sought to encourage generosity and social responsibility with this carol, it also contains some comfort and encouragement for the Christian pilgrim. As master and page go forward together, we might think of our journey with Christ, and, as in the experience of these two characters, there is sometimes bitter weather to endure. Then we might be reminded of the words of the master to the page:

"Hither, page, and stand by me," and his injunction to "mark my footsteps."

Wenceslas and his page boy remind us that we are not alone on our journey, especially if we go out to help others, and that Jesus will not abandon us if we seek to walk in the path of compassion in which he leads us. This journey of faith may well take us into cold, inhospitable, even dangerous places. Wenceslas himself knew this, ultimately suffering martyrdom. As we walk in our master's footsteps, we must be aware that we are walking not only the path of truth and light and love, but also the way of the cross. Jesus himself said to his disciples, "If any want to become my followers, let them deny themselves and take up their cross daily and follow me" (Luke 9:23).

This is our calling, just as it was for the first disciples and for St. Stephen, the first Christian martyr, whose feast day it is today. At Christmas time we celebrate and rejoice over the good news revealed in the crib, but we also remind ourselves of the suffering of the saints in many places throughout history, and we praise God for their example, striving always to be generous in material things and in spirit.

Prayer
Holy Jesus, as we seek always to walk in your footsteps, caring for others and blessing those who are poor in body or in spirit, guide us by the example of your saints, and in the power of your Spirit fill us with compassion and generosity, for you are our friend and master, now and always. Amen.

In the beginning was the Word, and the Word was with God, and the Word was God. He was in the beginning with God. All things came into being through him, and without him not one thing came into being. What has come into being in him was life, and the life was the light of all people. The light shines in the darkness, and the darkness did not overcome it.

There was a man sent from God, whose name was John. He came as a witness to testify to the light, so that all might believe through him. He himself was not the light, but he came to testify to the light. The true light, which enlightens everyone, was coming into the world.
—John 1:1–9

Like a candle flame,
Flick'ring small
in our darkness,
Uncreated light
shines through infant eyes.

God is with us, alleluia,
God is with us, alleluia,
Come to save us, alleluia,
Come to save us, alleluia.
Alleluia.

Stars and angels sing,
yet the earth
sleeps in shadows;
can this tiny spark
set a world on fire?

Yet his light shall shine
from our lives,

Spirit blazing,
As we touch the flame
of his holy fire.

Words and music: Graham Kendrick (b. 1950)

Candles symbolize a prayer, or a wish, a hope for something
good, or even a way of handling pain—of burning it away
in a tiny blaze of light. Of course, pain and evil cannot simply be
burned away with a candle (if only it were so easy!), but lighting
one comforts many people. We must also remember the spirituality
of the paschal candle, the great Easter candle that symbolizes the
light of the risen Christ shining in the midst of the darkness of
sin. It burns at baptisms, and a smaller candle, lit from it, is given
to the newly baptized. Thus we are baptized not only into Jesus'
death but into his resurrection (Romans 6:3–5). At Christmas,
when at Bethlehem we welcome the light of the world, it is good
to be reminded of the final outcome as God's love blazes from the
cross and rises, unextinguished, on the third day. God is with us,
yes, and he has come to save us.

The singer and songwriter Graham Kendrick was evidently in
touch with this kind of spirituality when he wrote "The candle
song." The popularity and success of his worship music is a
phenomenon to be admired and celebrated. "The candle song"
was produced with a choir of boys, and, to a certain extent, is the
most traditional-sounding of the Christmas songs that Kendrick has
written. Using a boy choir evokes cathedral choristers and large
spaces, but doing so also reminds us that Jesus himself was a little
boy once, born vulnerable and cold, yet to be the light of the world.

Jesus the Son was in the beginning, and was with God, and was God, and is God. He came into the same world that his Father created, like a candle burning in a pitch-dark cave, but the glare of mercy was too much for many, who rejected him. Yet there are others who, then and now, recognize the light of God burning in Christ through the ages. This is the light of Christ begun with a little spark, setting the world on fire: Christ the same yesterday and today, the light shining from our lives in a blaze of glory, illuminating the gift of eternal, resurrection life. God is with us, Alleluia!

Prayer

God with us, God among us, God within us, shine from our lives with the glow of joy that filled your fatherly heart when your Son came into the world. As your heavenly light took human form and shone through the eyes of the baby Jesus, shine the light of your love through the dark glass of our vision, so that your word may always be a lamp to our feet and a light on our path. Amen.

The Coventry Carol

When Herod saw that he had been tricked by the wise men, he was infuriated, and he sent and killed all the children in and around Bethlehem who were two years old or under, according to the time that he had learned from the wise men. Then was fulfilled what had been spoken through the prophet Jeremiah: "A voice was heard in Ramah, wailing and loud lamentation, Rachel weeping for her children; she refused to be consoled, because they are no more."
—Matthew 2:16–18

Lullay, Thou little tiny Child,
By, by, lully, lullay.
Lullay, Thou little tiny Child,
By, by, lully, lullay.

O sisters too, how may we do,
For to preserve this day.
This poor youngling for whom we sing
By, by, lully, lullay.

Herod the king, in his raging,
Charged he hath this day.
His men of might, in his own sight,
All young children to slay.

That woe is me, poor Child for Thee!
And ever morn and day,
For thy parting neither say nor sing,
By, by, lully, lullay.

Words: from the "Pageant of the Shearmen and Taylors" (fifteenth century), possibly annotated by Robert Croo and later by Thomas Sharp, 1817
Music: Anonymous, 1591

The dramatic and emotionally engaging story of Herod's killing of the children is one that cannot fail to touch the heart of anyone who hears it. On this day, the church remembers those poor children—the Holy Innocents. It is often said that no matter how much we might disagree on some moral issues, there is no reasonable society that tolerates the torture of children. Yet it happens, often because adults are frightened of the children who are destined to follow them. Herod killed because these little babies were a threat to him, not because of who they were but because of what he feared one of them might become—a rival. Thus we must honor these poor children, for they, unwittingly, died in Christ's place. Jesus was the intended victim, but he escaped to Egypt with Mary and Joseph. He survived and became the man born to die as a victim for all of us, but not at that time and place, so soon after being revealed to the world. Thus by divine providence he was saved, and by human evil others were brutally and tragically murdered.

It is to the heritage of English literature that we look to cast some light on the famous and ancient Coventry Carol. Both the music and the text are from the "Pageant of the Shearmen and Taylors," a medieval mystery play from the set of plays that were regularly performed in that city. Mystery plays date back at least as far as the great English poet Geoffrey Chaucer, who died in 1400. His *Canterbury Tales*, while not mystery plays as such, owe a great deal to that tradition, whereby religious subjects and fables are blended together to create a mixture of entertainment and moral teaching.

Medieval literature and drama grew out of church devotion, and while mystery plays were often performed in the street, their material was invariably biblical in origin. Their main purpose was to bring the Bible alive to a population that enjoyed pageantry and could not read the texts for themselves. In Coventry, as elsewhere, it was often the trade guilds who would present a play, hence the surviving remains of the pageant of Shearmen and Taylors, who combined for such a dramatic purpose. Their pageant told the story of Christ's birth and childhood, beginning with the Annunciation (Luke 1) and concluding with the massacre of the Holy Innocents. In the cycle of plays, it was immediately followed by the Weavers' guild production, as they would act out the story of the purification of Mary, the presentation of Christ in the temple (Candlemas), and the story of the young Jesus with the teachers (Luke 2:41–50).

The Shearmen and Taylors' play includes this most tragic and brutal story, which, as we can imagine, lent itself to a certain dramatic effect on stage. Chaucer's Absolon in "The Miller's Tale" describes himself as an actor in such a play:

Sometyme, to shew his lightnesse and maistyre
He playeth Herodes on a scaffold hye.

The "scaffold" had nothing to do with executions, but was a temporary stage, sometimes even a cart, on which the drama would be enacted. Being outdoors, and given in the vernacular, the opportunity for extensive, even blasphemous elaboration on the plot, was possible. The furious Herod, demanding the deaths of the infants, would be portrayed in an exaggerated way, no doubt employing colorful language not fit for church!

The Coventry mystery cycle was one of the best-known and drew crowds (including the royal family) from all over the country to watch the series of ten plays that made up the cycle. We should never forget that just as we can think of current examples of this kind of barbarous behavior, so too could our sixteenth-century predecessors. Whichever century we look into, including our own, we find that the names and circumstances change, but the scenario does not. We live in a violent, cruel world in which human beings damage, maim, and kill one another with calculated spite or mindless violence. This is our world, and it is God's world. It is the same world into which God himself was born, and is only different today because Christ took human flesh and made a difference. He shows us another way, speaking words of comfort and hope to those many who remain wholly innocent of the terrible crimes committed against them either in God's name, or in direct challenge to his ways of light and peace.

Prayer

Father of the old and of the young, hear the cries of your children who wail for your mercy and judgment. Turn the hearts of the cruel and the selfish, and banish all fear of difference, race, and creed from our world. Where innocence is drowned and love blemished, shed the healing light of your salvation among friends and foes alike, for the sake of Jesus your beloved Son. Amen.

The childhood of Christ

Now after they had left, an angel of the Lord appeared to Joseph in a dream and said, "Get up, take the child and his mother, and flee to Egypt, and remain there until I tell you; for Herod is about to search for the child, to destroy him." Then Joseph got up, took the child and his mother by night, and went to Egypt, and remained there until the death of Herod. This was to fulfil what had been spoken by the Lord through the prophet, "Out of Egypt I have called my son."
—Matthew 2:13–15

Thou must leave thy lowly dwelling,
The humble crib, the stable bare,
Babe, all mortal babes excelling,
Content our earthly lot to share,
Loving father, loving mother,
Shelter thee with tender care!
Loving father, loving mother,
Shelter thee with tender care,
Shelter thee with tender care!

Blessed Jesus, we implore thee
With humble love and holy fear,
In the land that lies before thee,
Forget not us who linger here!
May the shepherd's lowly calling
Ever to thy heart be dear!
May the shepherd's lowly calling
Ever to thy heart be dear,
Ever to thy heart be dear!

Blest are ye beyond all measure,
Thou happy father, mother mild!
Guard ye well your heavn'ly treasure,
The Prince of Peace, the Holy Child!
God go with you, God protect you,
Guide you safely through the wild!
God go with you, God protect you,
Guide you safely through the wild,
Guide you safely through the wild!

Words and music: Hector Berlioz (1803–69). Text trans. Paul England

The story of the temporary exile of the holy family inspired Hector Berlioz' "Sacred Trilogy," *L'enfance du Christ* (The Childhood of Christ), which was first performed at the St. Eustache Church in Paris in 1854. It is an unusual work, because it does not conform to the structures of oratorio or opera, and yet it is dramatic and narrative throughout. Berlioz wrote the text as well as the music, creating a set of three portraits or tableaux (hence a sacred trilogy). He suggested that the three sections of the piece were like pages of an illuminated medieval manuscript, representing Herod's dream, the flight to Egypt, and the arrival at Sais in Egypt.

The first part, "Herod's Dream," opens with a narrator setting the scene, who reminds us that no sooner had Jesus been born than Herod was plotting a terrible crime, but Jesus' parents would be warned, even while they waited in their humble stable. The action begins with two soldiers, one of whom is called Polydorus. His job is to guard Herod, who is tormented by dreams of treachery. Then we meet Herod, who is so jumpy that he draws his sword. Polydorus informs him that some soothsayers have arrived, and they proceed to offer him loyal service and advice. Herod recounts his fears: "A child has been recently born who will overthrow your throne and power. . . ." The soothsayers then perform a series of cabbalistic rituals, communing with the spirits of the dead. Consequently they inform Herod that his voices are accurate: a child has indeed been born who will abolish his throne, but no one knows who it is. Thus they advise him to kill all newborn babies. Rather like Macbeth under the influence of witchcraft, Herod is instantly persuaded by evil logic, and he resolves to shed "rivers of blood." He will show no pity, nor feel remorse in allaying his own personal fears. Thus the infants of Jerusalem, Nazareth, and Bethlehem will fall to the sword.

Berlioz likened his work to that of the medieval manuscript illuminators, and we might also remember that although the scenes with Herod and the soothsayers were written hundreds of years after the medieval plays, they seem to have been influenced by them, as indeed they are by Berlioz' passion for Shakespeare.

The action moves to Bethlehem, where the young Jesus is portrayed feeding the lambs and scattering flowers on their straw, encouraged by his parents. Their idyll is interrupted by the arrival of angels who warn Mary and Joseph that they must flee to Egypt immediately. Mary and Joseph, both used to following the advice of angels, agree, asking them for strength and protection. The angels depart, singing "Hosanna."

The central tableau describes the flight to Egypt, opening with an overture and the delightful "Shepherds' Farewell," which is often heard on its own at carol services and concerts at Christmas-time. The holy family set off on their journey, and they rest by a spring of water. The narrator describes the scene of grass and flowers (in the middle of the desert!), and how the angels worship the Christ-child as he sleeps in the shade. The scene might remind us of Genesis 21:19, the story of mother and son Hagar and Ishmael, who are saved by a similarly miraculous springing up of water in the desert. Here the brief scene ends with angels singing "Alleluia."

The third and final part sees Mary, Joseph, and Jesus arrive at the ancient Egyptian city of Sais. Archaeologists say that it was in the western Egyptian delta, where there is still a village called Sa el-Hagar, a name which combines the ancient Egyptian name for the city ("Sa") with the Arabic word for "stone." This suggests that there was once an impressive city there with many stone buildings. There is no biblical warrant for assuming that the family went to this Roman-occupied city, but the assumption is not so far-fetched. Berlioz's account of their arrival, exhausted, is moving and imaginative. The donkey has died in the desert, and they would not have survived, says the narrator, unless God had given them strength. The locals are not welcoming, however, which causes them further anguish.

Joseph knocks on the door of a house, seeking help, refuge, and rest, yet, with words that are often delivered to homeless people today, Joseph is told that he is not wanted. "Away with you," the residents say. Mary has bleeding feet, and no more milk, but they are similarly turned away elsewhere. Here is a foretaste of rejections that Jesus will experience in later life (Luke 9:51–55). Eventually they come to the home of an Ishmaelite, who is kind and admits them, and, rather like the Good Samaritan, puts all his resources at their disposal. Their feet are bathed and food and comfort are provided. The Ishmaelite man tells them that the children of Ishmael are brothers to the

Israelites, a phrase that resonates today as Christians, Jews, and Muslims alike strive to live together, sharing a common heritage but with different beliefs and traditions. The holy family can at last sleep safely and peacefully, happy in what will be their new home.

Thus, says the narrator, an unbeliever saved Jesus' life, and he tells us that he stayed there for ten years. Then, having developed a sublime, sweet, wise, and tender character, Jesus and his family returned to Nazareth, which he left to make the perfect sacrifice that saved humanity and opened the way to salvation. The Chorus concludes the story with an injunction to us all: what more can we do in the light of such a mystery than to be filled with the pure love that opens for us the gate of heaven?

Jesus was effectively homeless for a while. From an early age, the Son of Man had nowhere to lay his head, and from this we are also reminded that, like Christ, "we have no lasting city, but we are looking for the city that is to come" (Hebrews 13:14). We are all rootless without God, and, even as his followers, we wander on our pilgrimage until we reach our heavenly home.

Prayer

Father God, as we remember the poverty and defenselessness of your beloved holy family, feed us with the truth of your gospel and the power of your Spirit, that we may be ever vigilant for the homeless, the abandoned and the destitute, so that all your children may live with dignity and hope until your kingdom come. Amen.

December 30 **In the bleak midwinter**

Let the same mind be in you that was in Christ Jesus, who, though he was in the form of God, did not regard equality with God as something to be exploited, but emptied himself, taking the form of a slave, being born in human likeness. And being found in human form, he humbled himself and became obedient to the point of death—even death on a cross. Therefore God also highly exalted him and gave him the name that is above every name, so that at the name of Jesus every knee should bend, in heaven and on earth and under the earth, and every tongue should confess that Jesus Christ is Lord, to the glory of God the Father.

—Philippians 2:5–11

In the bleak midwinter
Frosty wind made moan,
Earth stood hard as iron,
Water like a stone;
Snow had fallen, snow on snow,
Snow on snow,
In the bleak midwinter,
Long ago.

Our God, heav'n cannot hold him
Nor earth sustain;
Heaven and earth shall flee away
When he comes to reign:
In the bleak midwinter
A stable-place sufficed
The Lord God Almighty,
Jesus Christ.
Enough for him, whom Cherubim

Worship night and day,
A breastful of milk,
And a mangerful of hay:
Enough for him, whom angels
Fall down before,
The ox and ass and camel
Which adore.

Angels and archangels
May have gathered there,
Cherubim and Seraphim
Thronged the air;
But only his mother
In her maiden bliss
worshiped the Beloved
With a kiss.

What can I give him,
Poor as I am?
If I were a shepherd
I would bring a lamb;
If I were a wise man
I would do my part;
Yet what I can I give him,
Give my heart.

Words: Christina Rossetti (1830–94)
Music: CRANHAM, Gustav Holst (1874–1934)

Christina Rossetti was overshadowed in her own time by her brothers' paintings and writings. Only a few of her poems were published in her lifetime, and "In the bleak midwinter" had a humble origin that today seems strangely fitting, since, like the Christ-child she describes, a humble beginning can lead to international fame and glory. If Christina Rossetti is famous for one thing, it is probably this carol.

She wrote it in 1872 in response to a request from a magazine called *Scribner's Monthly* for a Christmas poem. The poem did not find its way into any hymn book until after her death, being first published in *The English Hymnal* in 1906, in which Gustav Holst's hauntingly melancholic tune was paired with it. Christina Rossetti probably never heard this carol sung, neither to Holst's tune nor to a tune composed by Harold Darke in 1911. This later version is set for soloists with choral and organ accompaniment, and captures a very similar flavor of gentleness and awe, especially in the last verse where the choir is intended to evoke a chorus of quietly humming angels. In liturgical use, the carol serves very well indeed as an offertory hymn at a midnight or Christmas Day communion service, because of its clear evocations of Christ's humility and offering of himself, contrasted with the response we might make: "All things come from God, and of his own do we give him."

Rossetti's words have a piety and sweetness to them that always appeal at Christmas, but they also express some crucial truths about the birth of our Lord. She speaks of a bleak midwinter, and as we are often told that many people die over the Christmas period because of the cold, it is very easy for us to have a sense of what she means. And yet, the bleakness of the midwinter can have a spiritual meaning too, for it was to a cold, hard earth that Christ came, to be met with coldness of heart and rejection throughout his life before finally being executed on a cross.

The second verse indicates Christ's submission to earthly life in order to be born in that filthy, cold stable. Heaven cannot hold him, because God is bursting to redeem us; yet earth, the domain of sin, could not hold him, preferring to reject him: "He was despised and rejected by others; a man of suffering and acquainted with infirmity; and as one from whom others hide their faces he was despised, and we held him of no account" (Isaiah 53:3). There is irony in the fact that when Christ returns to reign, both heaven and earth will be subsumed in a new heaven and earth (Revelation 21:1–7). For now, though, as Christ is born among us, a dingy stable will do.

Only the most basic of human needs was met in that stable: a bed of hay and mother's milk. Christ's humility is revealed in the fact that as the firstborn of creation (Colossians 1:15), worshiped in heaven by angels and on earth only by beasts of burden, he took our flesh in conditions that even the people of his own day would have considered too lowly (Philippians 2:5–8).

We must not forget the activity of that most important human being in our Lord's life: his mother Mary. Divinity and humanity are nicely contrasted and combined in the fourth verse as Rossetti tells us that even though all the angels of heaven may have turned up to witness and pay homage at Christ's birth, there was one human being, Mary, who uniquely adored her child in that most tender of ways. Sweet, even over-romanticized as this image may be for some, it does remind us of the contrast between ethereal spirituality and physical humanity, which were brought together in that stable and for the next 30 years or so. Heavenly bodies don't kiss people, but real, loving human beings do.

That stable might remind us of the world in which we live, then and now—a cold, hard-hearted place. But we can also detect some physical warmth, in human love and basic creature comforts. Because of that very birth, warmth of heart and cleanliness from sin has come into the world, so much that even now, two millennia later, Christ's birth is still associated with generosity, good will, and rejoicing. Thus, as we reach the last verse, we find the heart of the matter, and an acknowledgment that God's gift of Christ to us demands a response: "What can I give him, poor as I am?"

Prayer

Poor as we are, O God, we offer you ourselves. Make of us what you will; use us to your glory. Humble us, exalt us, fill us, deprive us, only let us play our part in the hastening of your kingdom, so that when you come to reign, Father, Son, and Holy Spirit, our hearts may suffice as offerings to you. Amen.

*Long ago God spoke to our ancestors in many and various ways by
the prophets, but in these last days he has spoken to us by a Son,
whom he appointed heir of all things, through whom he also created
the world. He is the reflection of God's glory and the exact imprint of
God's very being, and he sustains all things by his powerful word.
When he had made purification for sins, he sat down at the right hand
of the Majesty on high, having become as much superior to angels as
the name he has inherited is more excellent than theirs. For to which
of the angels did God ever say, "You are my Son; today I have begotten you"? Or again, "I will be his Father, and he will be my Son"?
And again, when he brings the firstborn into the world, he says, "Let
all God's angels worship him."*
—Hebrews 1:1–6

Come then, only your name will be in my heart!
Thus I will call upon you, filled with delight,
When heart and breast burn for love of you.
But, my beloved, tell me,
How do I praise you, how do I thank you?
Jesus, my joy and bliss, my hope, treasure and reward,
My redeemer, defense and salvation,
Shepherd and King, light and sun!
Ah! How can I offer you worthy praise, my Lord Jesus?

Words: attributed to Christian Friedrich Henrici (also known as Picander)
(1700–64)
Music: J. S. Bach (1685–1750)

Many people regard the German composer Johann Sebastian Bach as the greatest composer of sacred music, and we should not overlook him in this book. The main reason that there is so much religious music by Bach is that he spent his working life writing music for liturgical services, first in Weimar, then Cothen, and finally as Cantor of St. Thomas, Leipzig, where he was appointed in 1723 and stayed until his death in 1750. The job involved teaching Latin and music at the church school, playing the organ, training the choir, hiring orchestral players and singers, and composing music for worship. His Passions, written while in Leipzig, are well-known and justifiably famous extended treatments of the passion narratives of St. John, St. Matthew, and St. Mark (long lost, but recently recreated), but there were other oratorios, and cantatas for each Sunday of the year, including Easter, Ascension, and Christmastide.

The oratorios are basically collections of cantatas, such that the Christmas Oratorio is actually a joining together of the cantatas that the fifty-year-old Bach composed for the period between Christmas and Epiphany 1734–35. Each of Bach's six cantatas opens with a chorus or sinfonia (instrumental piece), serving as a call to worship. The second section in each case is a setting of the appointed biblical text, sung by the character of the Evangelist (Gospel writer). The dramatic feel of each cantata is created by soloists tackling the various roles of the key characters, such as the Angel and Herod. The choir contributes by singing the parts of the heavenly host, the shepherds, the Magi, and the King of the Jews in the last part. Such an approach is very similar to that taken by Bach in his *Passions*, or indeed by Handel in his *Messiah*.

The text for the day, concerning the shepherds, Herod, or the presentation of Christ, forms a sort of keynote from which all else follows. The choruses, chorales, and arias that make up the rest of these cantatas are biblical reflections dramatized musically. Thus, in the fourth cantata the text is Luke 2:21: "After eight days had passed, it was time to circumcise the child; and he was called Jesus, the name given by the angel before he was conceived in the womb." It is preceded by a chorus in which we are entreated to "fall down with praise" and followed by a prayer of adoration, sung by a bass soloist:

Emmanuel, oh sweet word!
My Jesus is my shepherd,
My Jesus is my life.
My Jesus has given himself to me,
My Jesus will always
Hover in my sight.
My Jesus is my joy,
My Jesus restores heart and breast.

Chorales were introduced into church services by Martin Luther to enable the congregation to take part in and engage with music in worship. Chorales are like hymns: their straightforward tunes were harmonized by the choir or organ, and Bach's congregations would have learnt and sung the chorales that he used in the Christmas Oratorio. Sometimes a chorale melody is used in other movements, elaborated upon and carried beyond its simple origin.

In the final chorale of Part IV, the singers and congregation sing:

Jesus direct my beginning,
Jesus remain ever near me,

Jesus curb my senses,

Jesus be my only desire,

Jesus, remain in my thoughts always,

Jesus, never let me falter!

Such a conclusion seems appropriate as we end the year, reminding ourselves that although Jesus was born as one of us, it is our new birth in him that brings us salvation and happiness. As we turn the page on this year, and continue our journey into the next, let us remember our own beginnings but also anticipate our own death, not with fear and loathing, but with quiet delight in the name of Jesus who turns our earthly endings into new beginnings in his kingdom!

Prayer

God and Father of our Lord Jesus Christ, he is exalted as your Son, yet humbled himself to take on human nature, being born among us and dying for us. As another year draws to a close, help us to bid farewell to the year that is past, and greet tomorrow with hope and faith renewed. Amen.

What child is this?

In the time of King Herod, after Jesus was born in Bethlehem of Judea, wise men from the East came to Jerusalem, asking, "Where is the child who has been born king of the Jews? For we observed his star at its rising, and have come to pay him homage." When King Herod heard this, he was frightened, and all Jerusalem with him; and calling together all the chief priests and scribes of the people, he inquired of them where the Messiah was to be born. They told him, "In Bethlehem of Judea; for so it has been written by the prophet: 'And you, Bethlehem, in the land of Judah, are by no means least among the rulers of Judah; for from you shall come a ruler who is to shepherd my people Israel.'"
—Matthew 2:1–6

What child is this, who, laid to rest
On Mary's lap is sleeping?
Whom angels greet with anthems sweet,
While shepherds watch are keeping?
This, this is Christ the King,
Whom shepherds worship and angels sing:
Haste, haste to bring him praise,
The Babe, the son of Mary.

Why lies he in such mean estate,
Where ox and ass are feeding?
Come, have no fear, God's son is here,
His love all loves exceeding:
Nails, spear, shall pierce him through,
The cross be borne for me, for you:
Hail, hail, the Savior comes,
The Babe, the son of Mary.

So bring him incense, gold, and myrrh,
All tongues and peoples own him,
The King of kings salvation brings,
Let every heart enthrone him:
Raise, raise your song on high
While Mary sings a lullaby,
Joy, joy, for Christ is born,
The Babe, the son of Mary.

Words: W. Chatterton Dix (1837–98)
Music: English traditional

GREENSLEEVES, the tune of this delightful carol, is one of the most famous English song tunes, and has even been attributed to King Henry VIII. Shakespeare mentions it twice in *The Merry Wives of Windsor*, and the Worshipful Company of Stationers described it as being "new" in 1582. It may well be older than this, and was used liturgically long before the nineteenth century when William Chatterton Dix wrote the words we have here.

"What child is this?" was first published in Bramley and Stainer's *Christmas Carols, New and Old* in 1871. Dix's carol retells the story of Christmas in a rather unusual question and answer form.

The question "What child is this . . . ?" opens the carol, and there are various answers given. First, the child asleep in Mary's lap is indeed her son: "the babe, the Son of Mary." This fact is reiterated at the end of each verse. Whatever else we may say about this child, all appears normal and natural, a baby asleep. The gentle lilt of GREENSLEEVES, manifested in the 6/8 rhythm (two sets of three notes in a bar), musically portrays the rocking motion that parents use to get their little ones to sleep. But Dix's slightly sentimental opening, with sleeping child, angels singing, and shepherds watching has a stronger line to push as we progress through the carol. Be afraid, Dix warns us, be very afraid, for this silent, sleeping child, though he be the son of Mary, is the Word made flesh. The ever-so-human description of verse one is giving way to the theological meaning of this baby, of whom we may well ask, "What child is this?"

It may not have been deliberate on Dix's part, but he has in a sense caught something of the fundamental sense of alienation that we experience when faced with a newborn infant. He or she is related to the parents, of course, but to look on a newborn is not only to encounter someone beautiful and magical and joyous, but it is also about peering into depths of strangeness and mystery. Thus, when we ask of any baby, or even of any person, "Who is this?" we might simply be asking their name, expecting an obvious, simple answer, such as "This is Gordon" or "This is Maria." At the same time there is a more profound question lurking underneath: "Who are we, where did we come from, where are we going?" In this carol, there are elements of this ambiguity of questioning, so blithely disguised by a familiar and slightly sentimental tune.

On this eighth day after Christmas, we recall the naming and circumcision of Jesus, described in Luke 2:21: "After eight days had passed, it was time to circumcise the child; and he was called Jesus, the name given by the angel before he was conceived in the womb." This was a simple ceremony, but this was no ordinary little boy. We can ask questions about Jesus, sticking to the sentimental, shallow answers, or we can peer deeper, attempting to explore the significance of the Word made flesh, of Christ our king, and the way in which Mary's baby son can be both of these. While the choice is ours, here in this carol at least we can never avoid the sense that there is more than humanity being described here. And if we can grasp the dual nature of this human-divine child, asleep in Mary's arms but also awake to the sin of the world, then we too will wish to make haste to "bring him praise" and raise his song on high!

Prayer

Christ our baby Lord, whose name is above all names, and before whom every knee shall bow, may we grow to understand the meaning of your incarnation and the power of your self-giving arrival in our fragile world. Grant us simplicity of devotion and depth of insight, so that we may never trivialize your love for us, nor lose that sense of mystery that fills and fuels our journey of faith. Amen.

*On the fourteenth day they rested and made that a day of feasting and
gladness. . . . Therefore the Jews of the villages, who live in the open
towns, hold the fourteenth day of the month of Adar as a day for
gladness and feasting, a holiday on which they send gifts of food to
one another. Mordecai recorded these things, and sent letters to all the
Jews who were in all the provinces of King Ahasuerus, both near and
far, enjoining them that they should keep the fourteenth day of the
month Adar and also the fifteenth day of the same month, year by
year, as the days on which the Jews gained relief from their enemies,
and as the month that had been turned for them from sorrow into
gladness and from mourning into a holiday; that they should make
them days of feasting and gladness, days for sending gifts of food to
one another and presents to the poor.*
—Esther 9:17, 19–22

On the first day of Christmas my true love sent to me,
a partridge in a pear tree,
On the second day of Christmas my true love sent to me,
two turtle doves . . .
On the third day of Christmas my true love sent to me,
three French hens . . .
On the fourth day of Christmas my true love sent to me,
four calling birds . . .
On the fifth day of Christmas my true love sent to me,
five gold rings . . .
On the sixth day of Christmas my true love sent to me,
six geese a-laying . . .
On the seventh day of Christmas my true love sent to me,
seven swans a-swimming . . .
On the eighth day of Christmas my true love sent to me,
eight maids a-milking . . .

On the ninth day of Christmas my true love sent to me,
nine ladies dancing . . .
On the tenth day of Christmas my true love sent to me,
ten lords a-leaping . . .
On the eleventh day of Christmas my true love sent to me,
eleven pipers piping . . .
On the twelfth day of Christmas my true love sent to me,
twelve drummers drumming . . .

Words and music: Traditional

Some people have claimed that "The twelve days of Christmas" has its origins as a "catechism song," learnt by both children and adults as a way of preserving a coded knowledge of the faith. It is an attractive theory, which has gained popularity in America, but Christians in Britain hardly needed to encode the basic principles of Christianity, even during the Reformation or Commonwealth periods in the sixteenth and seventeenth centuries (while there was reformation of the church, Christianity was never itself outlawed). Also, as the song is a Christmas song, its use would have been somewhat limited. On the other hand, there are other encoded songs: "Sing a song of sixpence" is said to be about Henry VIII dissolving the monasteries, and "Ring around the rosy" is famously about the plague of 1665. Some commentators dispute this nowadays, making the radical claims that these songs are actually more or less about making pies and dancing in a circle! It always seems to be the case that where there is little fact to draw upon, speculation abounds, and whenever anyone comes up with a theory, someone else finds the means to refute it.

Therefore it is not entirely clear whether "The twelve days of Christmas" has a history of being a deep and meaningful spiritual song or not. It seems to have its origins in France, where three versions of the song are known, and also in an English question-and-answer type of song dating from around 1625, in which each of the days is given a religious significance. This song, called "A new dial" or "In those twelve days," would have been sung on Twelfth Night (January 6) as part of the festivities and games that accompanied that festival.

When "The twelve days of Christmas" was first published in 1780, it was presented as a singing game in which anyone who forgot a verse had to pay some kind of forfeit, such as kissing someone or performing some absurd action. The spirit of such parlor games is still very much with us, although Christmas afternoon television viewing may well have replaced these traditional festive games in most households. That "A new dial" and "The twelve days of Christmas" were part of games with seasonally appropriate religious themes may say more about the prevailing Christian culture of the time than it does about any desire to teach the tenets of the faith.

On the first day of Christmas, the true love sends a partridge in a pear tree. A tree in Christian symbolism has an obvious parallel in the tree of the cross: "Christ redeemed us from the curse of the law by becoming a curse for us—for it is written, 'Cursed is everyone who hangs on a tree'" (Galatians 3:13). The partridge gives us a clue to the French origin of the song, since partridges were first introduced into England from France in the late 1770s. Partridges, apparently, feign injury to protect their chicks. This might suggest that God, whom we take to be the true love, sent his Son Jesus on the first day of Christmas. We might also remember Jesus quoting 2 Esdras 1:30, in Luke 13:34: "I gathered you as a hen gathers her chicks under her wings." In art, the partridge has traditionally symbolized the church as the preserver of truth.

On the second day, we receive two turtle doves. It is a dove that settles on Jesus at his baptism (Mark 1:10). The presence of two doves reminds us of Jesus' presentation in the temple, where Mary and Joseph "offered a sacrifice according to what is stated in the law of the Lord, 'a pair of turtle doves or two young pigeons'" (Luke 2:24; see also Leviticus 1:14; 5:7; 12:6–8). The doves themselves might represent the two Testaments, Old and New, which together make up the Bible.

The third day brings us three French hens, which were expensive birds, especially in England. These might represent the three gifts of gold, frankincense, and myrrh brought by the magi to Jesus (Matthew 2:10–11). Three is a significant theological number, and so there are obvious overtones of the Trinity here. Jesus spent three days in the tomb. Another set of three might be the three virtues— faith, hope, and love—as presented by Paul in 1 Corinthians 13:13. The ancient Greek mathematician Pythagorus called three the "number of completion," because the beginning, the middle, and the end make up three parts.

The "four calling birds" of the fourth day of Christmas appears to be a corruption of "four colly birds." A colly bird is a blackbird, which presents us with a difficulty, as there is a legend about St. Benedict in which he is supposed to have been challenged by the devil in the form of a blackbird. Benedict recognized Satan and defeated him with the sign of the cross. It is perhaps better to remember that there are four Gospels, and think of each as calling out to us across time and space with the good news of Christ incarnate.

The five gold rings are not rings at all, but ringed pheasants. These birds appear in Fra Angelico's depiction of the nativity, painted around 1440. (We can now see, incidentally, that the first seven days of the song involve birds, while the last days involve people.) There are five books in the Pentateuch—the Mosaic law—and this verse may help us to remember that. There were also five wounds of Christ, which are often marked out on the paschal candle on Easter Eve: hands, feet, and side were all pierced during the crucifixion.

Just as the music of "The twelve days of Christmas" pauses on five gold rings, so we pause, completing this first part of our numerological foray into Christmas musical games.

Prayer

God our Father, who sent your true love Jesus Christ to be our light and salvation, fill us with the delight of serving you and of making your ways known upon earth. As we relish the joys of companionship, and admire the world in which you have placed us, help us always to remember that you are the creator and ruler of all things in heaven and earth. Amen.

A new dial: The twelve days of Christmas
Part Two

1) I believe in God, the Father almighty, creator of heaven and earth.
2) I believe in Jesus Christ, his only Son, our Lord. 3) He was conceived
by the power of the Holy Spirit and born of the virgin Mary. 4) He
suffered under Pontius Pilate, was crucified, died, and was buried. He
descended into hell [the grave]. 5) On the third day he rose again. He
ascended into heaven, and is seated at the right hand of the Father. 6)
He will come again to judge the living and the dead. 7) I believe in the
Holy Spirit, 8) the holy catholic Church, 9) the communion of saints,
10) the forgiveness of sins, 11) the resurrection of the body, 12) and
the life everlasting. Amen.
—The Apostles' Creed

In those twelve days let us be glad, in those twelve days let us be glad,
For God of his power hath all things made.
What are they but are but one?
One God, one baptism, and one faith, one truth there is,
the scripture saith:
What are they but are but two?
Two testaments, the old and new, we do acknowledge to be true:
What are they but are but three?
Three persons in Trinity which make one God in unity:
What are they but are but four?
Four sweet evangelists there are, Christ's birth, life, death,
which do declare:
What are they but are but five?
Five senses, like five Kings, maintain in every man a several reign:
What are they but are but six?
Six days to labor is not wrong, for God himself did work so long:

What are they but are but seven?
Seven Liberal Arts hath God sent down with divine skill
man's soul to crown:
What are they but are but eight?
Eight beatitudes are there given: use them aright and go to heaven:
What are they but are but nine?
Nine muses like the heavens' nine spheres, with sacred tunes
entice our ears:
What are they but are but ten?
Ten statutes God to Moses gave, which, kept or broke, do spill
or save:
What are they but are but eleven?
Eleven thousand virgins did partake, and suffered death for
Jesus' sake:
What are they but are but twelve?
Twelve are attending our God's Son: twelve make our Creed.
The dial's done.

Words: Collected by Davies Gilbert, 1822
Music: Traditional

Yesterday we began to look at "The twelve days of
Christmas," and today we continue. Picking up with the six
geese laying eggs, these may represent the six days of creation,
after which, on the seventh day, God rested (Genesis 1:24–31).
Eggs are often more associated with Easter, however, where they
are symbols of hope and resurrection, the chick breaking forth from
the shell just as Christ breaks forth in a new dawn of salvation. In
religious art, the goose is often associated with St. Martin of
Tours, for legend has it that it was a goose that gave away his

hiding place to those who wanted to appoint him bishop of that city in the fourth century. Even today, geese are used to guard property and to make a noise if anyone approaches, so we might associate them with spiritual vigilance as recommended in 1 Peter 5:8–9: "Discipline yourselves; keep alert. Like a roaring lion your adversary the devil prowls around, looking for someone to devour. Resist him, steadfast in your faith."

The swan does not appear to have any particular religious significance, although in England they were all the property of the Crown. Swans are associated in ancient Greek legends with the idea of a final "swansong," a cry that suggests they know that they are about to die. Thus they are sometimes associated with the gift of prophecy. There was also a belief that they could teach us the mysteries of music and poetry. The number seven may indicate the seven gifts of the Spirit from Romans 12:6–8: prophecy, ministry, teaching, exhortation, giving, leading, and compassion. The ancient hymn *Veni creator spiritus* refers to "thy sevenfold gifts," and there are many sevens in the book of Revelation. Seven is the number of perfection, a divine number. There are seven sacraments (eucharist, baptism, confirmation, ordination, unction, penance, and marriage), and seven deadly sins: greed, avarice, envy, gluttony, lust, sloth, and anger.

As we reach the eighth day, we abandon the birdcage for persons of diverse social standing, beginning with eight milkmaids. Eight is often associated with the resurrection, as Christ rose on the eighth day. This is why some baptismal fonts are octagonal. The significance of milkmaids is not clear, although we might be reminded of the apostle Paul's words: "I fed you with milk, not solid food, for you were not ready for solid food" (1 Corinthians 3:2). Just as milk is the basic source of food and life, provided at the mother's breast, so is the gospel the nourishment of our souls.

Nine can refer to the fruit of the Spirit described in Galatians 5:22–23. These are love, joy, peace, patience, kindness, generosity, faithfulness, gentleness, and self-control. That the nine ladies dance might remind us of Miriam dancing in Exodus 15:20–21. Spiritual dancing, although it has recently become more popular, has for centuries been viewed with some suspicion. In Exodus 32:19 it is dancing that makes Moses destroy the tablets of the Ten Commandments, and in Judges 11:34 we hear of Jepthah's unfortunate daughter dancing out to meet him.

Individual cases aside, dancing is an expression of joy and delight and, appropriately directed, such dancing can be a celebration of the abundant gift of life that Christ brings us. The ten leaping lords remind us of the Ten Commandments. "I am the Lord your God, who brought you out of the land of Egypt, out of the house of slavery," says the first commandment; "you shall have no other gods before me" (Exodus 20:2–3). Jesus sometimes criticized the Jewish leaders because they behaved as though the law were their God, as though they had ten "Lords," almost. The Ten Commandments are the basis of the Jewish faith, and therefore are also paramount in Christianity (Jesus never denounced them, but rather sought to uphold them). In John 13:34 Jesus gives us a new, eleventh commandment: " . . . that you love one another. Just as I have loved you, you also should love one another."

Eleven pipers are taken to represent the eleven named disciples who remained faithful to Christ after the betrayal by Judas. Later, Matthias was appointed by the casting of lots (Acts 1:22–26). Finally, there are a dozen drummers banging away. We might want to associate twelve with the apostles (but see "eleven"), or with the twelve tribes of Israel: Reuben, Simeon, Levi, Judah, Issachar, Zebulun, Benjamin, Dan, Naphtali, Gad, Asher, and Joseph. "A new dial" prefers twelve as defining sections of the Apostles' Creed. These twelve statements articulate Christian belief: they are the drumbeat of faith.

Today, "The twelve days of Christmas" can be useful precisely for the purpose that many doubt it originally had. These humorous, memorable lines still lend themselves as a teaching aid in an age that may have forgotten some of the basics of faith, if it ever knew them. At Christmas-time, when many people make a rare appearance in church, there may well be a place for this rather odd Christmas nursery rhyme.

The key, of course, lies in its numerological structure. Each numbered day has a resonance with something numerical in our faith, and it is not hard to remember, discover or even invent a connection.

Prayer

O Lord, to whom all shall give account, number us among your chosen people, fill us with the vision of eternity, and grant that we may turn to you each hour of every day, ever inspired by the range and depth of your love revealed in creation and in the saving work of Jesus Christ, your Son, our Lord. Amen.

Tomorrow shall be my dancing day

For everything there is a season, and a time for every matter under heaven: a time to be born, and a time to die; a time to plant, and a time to pluck up what is planted; a time to kill, and a time to heal; a time to break down, and a time to build up; a time to weep, and a time to laugh; a time to mourn, and a time to dance; a time to throw away stones, and a time to gather stones together; a time to embrace, and a time to refrain from embracing; a time to seek, and a time to lose; a time to keep, and a time to throw away; a time to tear, and a time to sew; a time to keep silence, and a time to speak; a time to love, and a time to hate; a time for war, and a time for peace. . . . He has made everything suitable for its time; moreover, he has put a sense of past and future into their minds, yet they cannot find out what God has done from the beginning to the end.
—Ecclesiastes 3:1–8, 11

Tomorrow shall be my dancing day:
I would my true love did so chance
To see the legend of my play,
To call my true love to my dance:
    Sing, O my love,
    This have I done for my true love.

In a manger laid and wrapped I was,
So very poor this was my chance,
Betwixt an ox and a silly poor ass,
To call my true love to my dance:

Then was I born of a virgin pure,
Of her I took fleshly substance;

Thus was I knit to man's nature,
To call my true love to my dance:

Then afterwards baptized I was;
The Holy Ghost on me did glance,
My Father's voice heard from above,
To call my true love to my dance:

Words and music: Traditional
Also music: John Gardner (b. 1917)

As we hinted yesterday, dance has had a chequered spiritual history, during which it has often been alienated, proscribed, or at best ignored. The Prayer Book of 1549 drawn up by Archbishop Thomas Cranmer had a motif of the "Dance of Death" as an illustration alongside the psalms, and the artist Hans Holbein created a series of woodcut drawings in 1538 which include "The alphabet of Death," in which each letter has a morbid theme. In another picture, "The new-married lady," the character of Death insidiously dances before the bride and groom, beating a tambour. Old St. Paul's Cathedral, destroyed in the great London fire of 1666, had similarly macabre carvings lining the cloisters, illustrating sinister verses written by the pöet John Lydgate, who was a contemporary of Chaucer.

More recently, the French composer Camille Saint-Saëns (1835–1921) wrote his famous *Danse Macabre* in which the plainsong tune to the Dies Irae (part of the Latin funeral service) forms the musical theme, with xylophones illustrating rattling bones while "Death" retunes his violin, creating a weird and wonderful clash representing the discord between the worlds of the living and the dead.

But it is not all bad news for Christian devotees of dance, for in opposition to the Dance of Death, we might consider the "Dance of Life," which also has a long history. Many people are familiar with the hymn "Lord of the dance," written in 1963 by Sidney Carter. The hymn's origins in folk music are clear: the tune that Carter used comes from the American Appalachian mountain region ("'Tis a gift to be simple"), which the composer Aaron Copland also used in his orchestral work *Appalachian Spring*. What is perhaps not so well known is the tradition from which Carter's hymn wells up. "Lord of the dance" owes a great deal of homage to a much older carol called "Tomorrow shall be my dancing day," which also characterizes the story of Christ's life as a kind of dance.

The text of "Tomorrow shall be my dancing day" was first published in 1833, but almost certainly has its origin in the medieval mystery plays, which often ended with a processional dance. The actor playing Christ would sing the verses, and actors and audience would dance and sing during the refrain. It was also not unusual for the character of the baby Jesus to sing a song foretelling his life, mission, and purpose. Thus the carol actually has twelve verses in total, although the four reproduced here are the ones most often heard today. Other verses tell of the temptations in the wilderness, the betrayal by Judas, the trials and scourging by Pilate, the crucifixion and piercing, the descent to hell and the resurrection and ascension. As a result, there is a sense in which this carol could be used throughout the year, although it has been saddled with a Christmas flavor and is therefore neglected. It is perhaps a little strange that we move so quickly from the visit of the magi to the baptism of Christ, but this carol reminds us that in Scripture the account of the baptism of Christ does more or less follow that of the birth narratives. During the season of Epiphanytide, between January 6 and February 2 (Candlemas), it is good to reflect on those three "revealings" of Christ: his encounter with the magi, his baptism, and the turning of water into wine at Cana (John 2:1–11).

While the carol itself may have medieval origins, the idea of Christ as "my true love" not only reminds us of "The twelve days of Christmas" but also carries us back to the Song of Songs, the love poetry of the Old Testament, the rich and suggestive language of which has often been treated as allegorical, representing the union between Christ and the church. "Tomorrow shall be my dancing day" is not only a love song, it is also a wedding dance, hinting at an intimacy between Christ and church that takes as its model the human experience of loving relationship.

While the relationship between dance and faith has not always been a good one, Christmas and Easter carols such as "Lord of the dance" and "Tomorrow shall be my dancing day" have brought the two together in a popular and accessible way.

Just as there is a time to be born and a time to die, so there are liturgical events to mark those crucial and inevitable moments of joy or grief. Such situations are by no means only to be found in the distant past, but arise in each and every generation.

We find these fundamental truths of human existence to which Ecclesiastes refers in any period of time, past or present, and yet, as he reminds us, we "cannot find out what God has done from the beginning to the end" (3:11). Life, with all its ups and downs, dances and sorrows, is still a great mystery to us. But in its diversity and regularity is to be found something of God, our creator, our redeemer, our sustainer, who partners us in the dances of both life and death, leading us onward and upward to our heavenly rest.

Prayer

Jesus, you are Lord of the dance and victor over death. Help our souls to dance to the music of your mercy, and our hearts to beat to the rhythms of your praise, so that at any time and in every place we may be ever mindful that you are the same yesterday, today, and tomorrow. Amen.

Ahmal and the Night Visitors

Then Jesus, filled with the power of the Spirit, returned to Galilee, and a report about him spread through all the surrounding country. He began to teach in their synagogues and was praised by everyone. When he came to Nazareth, where he had been brought up, he went to the synagogue on the sabbath day, as was his custom. He stood up to read, and the scroll of the prophet Isaiah was given to him. He unrolled the scroll and found the place where it was written: "The Spirit of the Lord is upon me, because he has anointed me to bring good news to the poor. He has sent me to proclaim release to the captives and recovery of sight to the blind, to let the oppressed go free, to proclaim the year of the Lord's favor." And he rolled up the scroll, gave it back to the attendant, and sat down. The eyes of all in the synagogue were fixed on him. Then he began to say to them, "Today this scripture has been fulfilled in your hearing." All spoke well of him and were amazed at the gracious words that came from his mouth. They said, "Is not this Joseph's son?"

—Luke 4:14–22

I n 1951, the Italian composer Gian Carlo Menotti (b. 1911) was asked by the National Broadcasting Company (NBC) to compose the first opera written especially for television, to be broadcast in the United States on Christmas Eve that year. The task was certainly a daunting one: the idea that millions of people might be watching does not trouble Olympic athletes and newsreaders today, but it is so easy for us to forget (if we are old enough!) what the early days of television were like. Even as November began, Menotti had not the first idea what to write about. The solution was to be found in a painting attributed to Hieronymus Bosch, "The Adoration of the Magi," which he saw in the Metropolitan Museum of Art in New York. It depicts, kneeling before the Madonna and child, not only three wise men but also peasants and curious onlookers. As far as Menotti was concerned, the three kings in this painting brought him a gift—the inspiration for a successful and popular hour-long opera called *Ahmal and the Night Visitors*.

The story is that of a young boy who lives with his mother. She is very poor, and he cannot walk without a crutch. One night, the three magi visit them on their way to Bethlehem. Ahmal is astonished, and his mother does not believe him when he tells her that there is a king at the door. She knows he has a vivid imagination, and accuses him of fibbing. Twice he returns, admitting his error: there is not a king at the door, but two kings ... and then three! The kings are not only bearing gifts; they also bring with them a wondrous story, a tale of the birth of a Savior whom they intend to visit.

Ahmal's mother is awed and humbled, and she sends her son to tell the local shepherds, who soon appear offering food, for which the kings are grateful. Then the shepherds dance, accompanied by Ahmal, playing his shepherd's pipes. Menotti portrays their dancing as at first hesitant, betraying their nervousness, but becoming more confident as the music builds to a whirling tarantella. (A tarantella is an Italian dance, fast and furious, which one supposedly dances after having been bitten by a tarantula spider!)

After the excitement and dancing, everyone turns in for the night except Ahmal's mother, who lies awake, troubled by how much even one of those gifts might help her poor crippled son. Tormented into action, she steals some gold. She is caught, however, and berated by the kings. Meanwhile, Ahmal wakes up and tries to help his terrified mother by rushing to her aid, crying, "Don't you dare hurt my mother!" King Melchior forgives her attempted theft, and says that the child they are looking for hardly needs gold anyway. Instead, he tells her, Jesus will build his kingdom on love, and the keys of his city belong to the poor. "He will soon walk among us," Melchior sings, and "He will bring us new life and receive our death."

These words touch the mother's heart, and in spite of being offered the gold she tried to take, she now rejects it, saying that she has waited so long for such a child as they describe, and she would send a gift of her own if only she could. Ahmal interjects, suggesting that they send Jesus his crutch ("who knows, he may need one," he sings). His mother says that he can't do such a thing, but a miracle has begun. As Ahmal raises his crutch to offer it as a gift to send to Bethlehem, he realizes that he doesn't need it any more. The kings and their page are in awe of Ahmal now, and want to touch him, because he has been touched by God. Ahmal says he wants to go to Bethlehem too, so that he can give thanks to the holy child who has evidently healed him. His mother agrees, and they depart, Ahmal playing his pipes as they recede into the snowy landscape.

This delightful story, with its English text and accessible music, has found a central place in the Christmas repertoire, especially in the United States. Melody abounds in this straightforward opera, and Menotti himself said that he saw Ahmal as a door-way into opera for children. The same could almost be said of its theology. Set out as a kind of fairy tale, it may seem light-weight theologically, and we might even be wary of the artistic license taken with the figures of the three kings (Matthew 2:1–12 does not specify kings, or that there were three of them). On the other hand, Menotti's treatment of these three characters, one of whom is portrayed as being rather deaf and a bit crazy, humanizes these magi from the mists of Matthew's Gospel, and children may well come to learn more of the real story that lies behind this folk-like tale. Nor is the story lacking in spiritual depth: its overall message speaks of good news for the poor and lame, forgiveness for transgressors, and of how charity and selfless love can lead to miracles, which in turn lead to praise and thanksgiving.

Although the work was a very successful experiment in television opera, Menotti was cautious about that medium, which the world now takes for granted. Writing a program note for a 1963 production, he wrote about those who watch television casually:

> The spectator who takes no journey and has no appointed time or seat, but, carelessly clad, sits casually on the first available chair in his living room, and who, knitting or perhaps playing with the kitten, "turns on" what he takes to be a theatrical performance, will never know the emotion of a real theatrical experience . . . (the artist) addresses you in utter dignity—whether his message be comic or tragic—and to partake in his experience, you must share this seriousness and receive his message wearing your "Sunday clothes."

The same might be said for worship. Menotti's words remind us that while we can project and receive our experiences of any-thing through almost any medium, there is a lot to be said for really partaking—for getting involved, being there, rather than simply being observers, judges, or spectators. Ahmal realizes this when he desires to go and thank the Christ-child himself. We watch Ahmal's mother struggle with her poverty, and we watch

Ahmal offer his crutch to Jesus, and we are moved—we feel involved. Worship, like art, is a two-way engagement. It is not a show, like something on television, which we can dip into, or play with at Christmas-time when all the nice carols get sung. Worship, like art, requires a bit of effort, and is not a spectator's exercise in observation. It is about relationship, with God and with those who also partake.

Prayer

O Lord Jesus Christ, you are the medium and the message of our salvation. We give you thanks and praise for the glorious mystery of your birth and the miracle of your incarnation. Inspire and assist us always to care for the poor and needy, and let us never lean on anything other than the hope and joy you bring us. Amen.

We three kings

Herod secretly called for the wise men and learned from them the exact time when the star had appeared. Then he sent them to Bethlehem, saying, "Go and search diligently for the child; and when you have found him, bring me word so that I may also go and pay him homage." When they had heard the king, they set out; and there, ahead of them, went the star that they had seen at its rising, until it stopped over the place where the child was. When they saw that the star had stopped, they were overwhelmed with joy. On entering the house, they saw the child with Mary his mother; and they knelt down and paid him homage. Then, opening their treasure-chests, they offered him gifts of gold, frankincense, and myrrh.

—Matthew 2:7–11

We three kings of Orient are;
Bearing gifts we traverse afar
Field and fountain, moor and mountain,
Following yonder star:
  O star of wonder, star of night,
  Star with royal beauty bright,
  Westward leading, still proceeding,
  Guide us to thy perfect light.

Born a king on Bethlehem plain,
Gold I bring, to crown him again—
King for ever, ceasing never,
Over us all to reign:

Frankincense to offer have I;
Incense owns a deity nigh:
Prayer and praising, all men raising,
Worship him, God most high:

Myrrh is mine; its bitter perfume
Breathes a life of gathering gloom;
Sorrowing, sighing, bleeding, dying,
Sealed in the stone-cold tomb:

Glorious now, behold him arise,
King, and God, and sacrifice!
Heav'n sings alleluya,
Alleluya the earth replies:

Words and music: J. H. Hopkins (1820–91)

"We three kings of orient are" is probably the best-known of all Epiphany carols. It is also the one that is most often brought forward into the Christmas season for use at carol services and in nativity plays. This is because it is so easy to learn and sing, and even very young children can manage the refrain. Furthermore, what we have here is a straightforward dramatization of the story of the wise men's visit to Jesus, as recounted in Matthew 2:1–11.

The carol was first published in 1884, and its author, the Rev. Dr. John Hopkins, was Rector of Williamsport in Pennsylvania. He wrote it as part of a Christmas pageant for the General Theological Seminary in New York City. Hopkins, composer of many carols and hymns, wrote both the words and the music, which is somewhat unusual. This does mean, however, that there are certain issues about this carol which we can lay squarely at his door! For example, the refrain begins "O . . . star of wonder . . . ," and while Hopkins was quite explicit that there should be no slowing down or dragging of the word "O," there is such a diversity of interpretation over the potential slowing up before each refrain, that the musicians leading have to give a very strong lead indeed—once they have made their own mind up, of course!

Any criticism of Hopkins' music must then give way to a recognition of his misleading text, the consequences of which have to be addressed every Christmas all over the English-speaking world. The simple fact is that those people who visited Christ from Eastern lands were not kings; nor were there three of them. Yet so many children, nurtured on this carol, carry into adult life this misconception so carelessly promulgated by the Rev. Dr. Hopkins. As a parish clergyman, he should have known better. . . .

Of course, he did know better, and if we look into the carol a bit more deeply, we discover that his use of "three kings" is quite deliberate and points us towards traditions other than the strictly biblical one. Origen (c. 185–c. 254) first suggested that there were three gift-bearers, largely because three gifts are mentioned and it was assumed from an early date that they brought one each. The tradition that they might have been kings is more complicated. A sixth-century tradition gives the "kings" the names of Caspar, Balthasar, and Melchior. These names are often used when "We three kings" is sung, and sometimes soloists take their roles. In some churches the drama is heightened further, with the carol being sung in procession around the building: as each "king" sings their verse, the related gift of gold, frankincense, or myrrh is presented at the crib or altar.

The origin of the kings' names comes from an ancient custom of blessing homes at the beginning of each year on the feast of the Epiphany. As with any Christian holy day, the observation of the feast may begin on the previous evening. According to a tradition that predates the Middle Ages, the Latin blessing

Christus mansionem benedicat ("May Christ bless this home") would be said, while the first letters of the words were inscribed above the doorway of the house. The chalk used for writing these letters, C-M-B, would have been previously blessed, and it is from this practice that we still find in some schools a tradition of blessing the chalk to be used during the year. Of course, in this age of eraserboards and marker pens, some of the historical significance is lost!

The names Caspar, Melchior, and Balthasar were invented as a memory aide for the blessing, and became inextricably associated with it. Thus in Germany, dried herbs would be burnt and their aroma would fill the house. Doorways would be sprinkled with holy water and the master of the house would write "CMB" and the year in chalk above the house and barn door, saying, "Caspar, Melchior, Balthasar, behütet uns auch für dieses Jahr, vor Feuer und vor Wassergefahr" ("Caspar, Melchior, Balthasar, protect us again this year from the dangers of fire and water").

Built into this ancient tradition is the idea of a new start and a new year. We begin our new year on January 1, of course, but New Year's Day falls in the midst of the Christmas season, and is itself known as the feast of the naming of Jesus. In societies and ages that were much more ecclesiastically minded than ours is now, it made far more sense to consider the feast of the Epiphany to be the end of one season and the beginning of another. In the West, Christmas was December 25 and Epiphany (the "revealing" of Christ) was January 6, twelve days later. This is why we speak of "twelve days of Christmas." Only when the twelve days are over is there really a sense of moving away from Christmas towards the recently welcomed new year. It is almost as if, on the last day of Christmas, the wise men not only bring gifts but they also herald the new year ahead. Christmas is over, and so we push on towards Candlemas and thence to Lent. (Candlemas is 40 days after Christmas, on February 2, and marks the celebration of Christ's presentation in the temple as recounted in Luke 2:22–38.)

So it is appropriate that we end our Christmas season here, saying farewell as the wise men greet Jesus. Their arrival fulfils the psalmist's prophecy: "May the kings of Tarshish and of the isles render him tribute, may the kings of Sheba and Seba bring gifts. May all kings fall down before him, all nations give him service. . . . Long may he live! May gold of Sheba be given to him" (Psalm 72:10–11, 15).

With Christmas now over, we can take down our Christmas trees and decorations, plunder the tree for goodies and look forward to the new term and the lengthening of the days. So let us end as we began. Let us be vigilant and watchful, waiting for our Lord and ensuring that Christmas never becomes less than what it truly is: the celebration of Christ's nativity, the welcoming, each year, of God made flesh, revealed among us, now and until the end of time.

Prayer

O King of kings and Lord of lords, who was born at Bethlehem and revealed to the nations as God among us, grant us a portion of your heavenly wisdom, that we may always be guided on our journey by the light of your salvation, shining for all the world to see. Amen.

Suggestions for group discussion or individual reflection

It is very common in churches these days to have Lent study courses, but Advent courses are probably less common. Nevertheless, the opportunities for fellowship, reflection and "time out" can be particularly valuable in the hectic pre-Christmas period. It is perhaps a very noble and fortunate group that is able to meet between Christmas and New Year, or between New Year and Epiphany, but an opportunity to reflect together at that time can help to ground us in the true meaning of the festivities.

In an attempt to be both realistic and encouraging in this respect, here are some topics and questions that might be used as the basis for a group meeting, or for personal reflection. Where groups use this material, it will be beneficial to add opening and closing prayers (offered at the end of each chapter), time for recapitulation of the previous week's issues and opportunity for sharing ideas and experiences.

First week of Advent Procession into Advent

1. Have you ever been to an Advent carol service? Describe what happened. What significance or relevance does the "procession of Advent" have today?
2. What is your impression of the ancient texts of Advent that are still in use today? To what extent do we only know them today because they have been preserved in musical works?
3. What do you think about the way hymn writers take Scripture and adapt it poetically? Should we regard an ancient hymn as equal to Scripture, or merely as a commentary upon it?

4. Think about your expectations and hopes for the coming month. In what way will you be or feel any different by the time we reach Christmas?
5. What is the point of Advent?

Sing or listen to "Lo! He comes with clouds descending."

Santa Claus
Begin by singing or listening to "Thou whose almighty word."
Read 1 Timothy 3.

1. What do you know about St. Nicholas? Do you approve of the way in which he has mutated into Santa Claus?
2. Should children be told that Santa Claus does (not) exist? Why? How can St. Nicholas help us with the mission and ministry of the church in this day and age?
3. If you can, listen to some (or all) of Britten's Cantata. How is this like the Santa Claus we know and love?
4. What do you want for Christmas? How do you react to being made to wait for things? (Can you wait for anything or are you like a child on Christmas Eve who cannot sleep for anticipation?)
5. What are we really waiting for? What do you really believe is going to happen?

Finish by prayerfully singing (or listening to) the Taizé chant "Wait for the Lord."

John and Justice
Begin by singing "Born in the night."
Read John 1:6–39.

1. Have a look at some of Raphael's paintings of Jesus with John the Baptist. How do they strike you?

(See www.abcgallery.com/R/raphael/raphael.html)
Reflect for a little while on the relationship between John
and Jesus throughout their young lives. In what sense is it
right to think of John as a Christian martyr (someone who
dies witnessing to the resurrection of Christ)?

2. Listen to Gibbons' "This is the record of John." What
impact does the use of a high male alto voice have? How
would John have come across to the people of his day?
How does he come across now?

3. Identify some situations today where issues of justice for
the poor and needy are still of concern. Reflect on the
response of aid from peoples and governments, such as in
December 2004 when the tsunami struck southeast Asia.
How do John's ascetic lifestyle and Jesus' humble birth
speak to these situations? How can we admire glorious
paintings and wonderful music when others suffer and perish
through natural or humanly created violence or disaster?

4. Is it realistic to suppose that Christ might walk in our
streets again—or how might he already be doing so?

Finish by listening to John Tavener's anthem "The Lamb."

Fourth week of Advent   **O Come, Emmanuel**
Begin by singing or listening to "O come, O come, Emmanuel."

1. Consider the Advent antiphons on which the verses are
based. What do they mean? Consider what they meant
when they were written, and what they might mean for us
today. Can you think of situations to which these antiphons
speak? For whom might they be helpful? What is going on
here—what are we calling on Christ to be for us, both here
and now and upon his return?

2. Christmas is approaching fast, and has been evident in the
shops for many weeks. Is our sense of anticipation coming

to an end? How can we prevent Christmas from being an anticlimax?

3. Listen to a setting of "Adam lay ybounden." What do you make of the text?
4. Read Genesis 3. Is it right to say that it was a good thing that Adam sinned because it enabled the incarnation, passion, and resurrection of Christ? Wouldn't it have been better if Adam and Eve had behaved themselves?
5. What would life be like if they had? What will it be like after Jesus returns? How would you explain Adam's sin and Christ's return to a non-Christian?

Finish by singing "Of the father's heart begotten."

Christmas week or New Year's week **Religion at Christmas**
Sing or listen to "Masters in this hall."

1. This whole period is part of the Christmas season, liturgically speaking. How pagan has your Christmas been? How can the traditions of light, mistletoe and dancing, indulgence and television be reconciled with the original and true meaning of the Incarnation?
2. Reflect on the Christmas cards you have sent or received (group members may like to bring along examples). What are the pictures saying? What are the greetings inside saying about the people who have sent them and the spirit in which they are sent? What do you really feel about the sending of Christmas cards: is it a good thing, a bad thing, or an inevitable chore?

Read Luke 1:26–56. Listen to a setting of the Ave Maria.

3. Does the Ave Maria appeal or does it annoy you? Reflect and pray about your response to it. What do you feel about religious conflict? Where are there religious conflicts happening around us now, and why? How can or should such

conflict be avoided? What does the Magnificat have to contribute to this debate?

Finish by singing a popular Christmas carol, such as "Hark! the herald angels sing."

Epiphany Week　　**Twelfth Night and Tomorrow**
Listen to or sing "The twelve days of Christmas."
Say the Apostles' Creed together.

1. What do you think about the idea that this song might have religious significance? Whether it was intended to or not, do you find numerological interpretations of it helpful, or are you happier with it as a simple folk-tune nonsense game?
2. If you want a bit of fun, try to rewrite the song, beginning with "On the first day of Christmas, Jesus gave to me. . . ."
3. Think about the power of music to influence opinion and change lives. Consider some contemporary writers: what contribution have Graham Kendrick, Taizé, and Iona made to our worshiping life?
4. How important is music in your life? Is Jesus your true love? Are the two connected in any way?
5. Read Matthew 2:1–11. Would you make such a journey? Is there an equivalent today? How is the debate about whether the magi were wise men, kings, or astrologers relevant today? What is the true meaning of Epiphany and why does it mark the beginning of a season that lasts nearly a month?
6. What will next Christmas be like? How do you think the world will have changed? How will you have changed?

Finish by listening to "Tomorrow shall be my dancing day,"
preferably John Gardiner's setting.

About Paraclete Press

Who We Are

Paraclete Press is an ecumenical publisher of books and recordings on Christian spirituality. Our publishing represents a full expression of Christian belief and practice—from Catholic to Evangelical, from Protestant to Orthodox.

Paraclete Press is the publishing arm of the Community of Jesus, an ecumenical monastic community in the Benedictine tradition. As such, we are uniquely positioned in the marketplace without connection to a large corporation and with informal relationships to many branches and denominations of faith.

We like it best when people buy our books from booksellers, our partners in successfully reaching as wide an audience as possible.

What We Are Doing
Books

Paraclete Press publishes books that show the richness and depth of what it means to be Christian. Although Benedictine spirituality is at the heart of all that we do, we publish books that reflect the Christian experience across many cultures, time periods, and houses of worship.

We publish books that nourish the vibrant life of the church and its people— books about spiritual practice, formation, history, ideas, and customs.

We have several different series of books within Paraclete Press, including the bestselling Living Library series of modernized classic texts; A Voice from the Monastery—giving voice to men and women monastics about what it means to live a spiritual life today; award-winning literary faith fiction; and books that explore Judaism and Islam and discover how these faiths inform Christian thought and practice.

Recordings

From Gregorian chant to contemporary American choral works, our music recordings celebrate the richness of sacred choral music through the centuries. Paraclete is proud to distribute the recordings of the internationally acclaimed choir Gloriæ Dei Cantores, who have been praised for their "rapt and fathomless spiritual intensity" by American Record Guide, and the Gloriæ Dei Cantores Schola, which specializes in the study and performance of Gregorian chant. Paraclete is also the exclusive North American distributor of the recordings of the Monastic Choir of St. Peter's Abbey in Solesmes, France, long considered to be a leading authority on Gregorian chant performance.

Learn more about us at our Web site:
www.paracletepress.com,
or call us toll-free at
1-800-451-5006.

Christmas Favorites from Paraclete Press

Sing Noel
with Gloriæ Dei Cantores

ISBN: 1-55725-229-7
$16.95, CD

Gloriæ Dei Cantores brings to life Ralph Hunter's exciting Christmas Medley *Sing Noel.* Brass and handbells enhance this Christmas album spanning two centuries of holiday favorites, including "A Flight of Angels," "Carol of the Friendly Beasts," "Away in a Manger," "Ding Dong Merrily on High," and more.

The First Christmas Tree and Other Stories
Henry Van Dyke

91 pages
ISBN: 1-55725-315-3
$15.95, Hardcover

For over one hundred years, the writings of Henry Van Dyke have been lovingly passed down from generation to generation. His Christmas stories, especially, are as resonant today as when this Presbyterian minister first read them to his New York City congregation in the late 1890s. In this volume of Christmas stories and prayers, we read of courage, generosity, and the triumph of light over darkness.

The Story of the Other Wise Man
Henry Van Dyke

94 pages
ISBN: 0-941478-33-5
$10.95, Paperback

What if there was another Wise Man who, unable to join the three, nonetheless embarked on the same quest? Searching for the Promised One, Artaban meets him at last—too late?